Baptist Spirituality

A Call for Renewed Attentiveness to God

BY E. GLENN HINSON

© 2013

Published in the United States by Nurturing Faith Inc., Macon GA,
www.nurturingfaith.net.

Library of Congress Cataloging-in-Publication Data is available.

ISBN 978-1-938514-28-9

This book is sponsored by the
COOPERATIVE BAPTIST FELLOWSHIP
MISSIONAL CONGREGATIONS INITIATIVE
Bo Prosser, Coordinator for Missional Congregations

Contents

Foreword

Glenn Hinson is one of my heroes and probably one of your heroes, too. He is one of those voices to whom I listen, not only because of the value of his insights, but also because he makes good sense. He is inspiring and thought-provoking, yet he is practical and purposeful. He is a historian, a contemplative, and definitely a wise man. That seems to qualify him as "hero" as far as I'm concerned.

The chapters that follow are based on the lectures he presented during a 5-Day Academy for Spiritual Formation co-sponsored by the Cooperative Baptist Fellowship and the Upper Room and held at the Ignatius House Retreat Center in Atlanta in October 2012. Through a combination of prayer lessons, worship, lectures, and intentional silence, a special community of more than forty people from several faith groups was forged.

Glenn delivered these lectures just a few weeks after having major heart bypass surgery! We prayed and hoped that he would be strong enough to attend and be able to present. And in true hero fashion, he was ready to teach at each appointed hour. While his stamina was understandably a bit low, his insights, inspiration, and passion for the work were at an all-time high. He continues to be relevant and masterful as he shares his unique blend of church history and spirituality.

He has definitely immersed himself in both disciplines. His words will bring to the reader equal measures of illumination, challenge, and affirmation. Many will know this master teacher only through his recent autobiography, *A Miracle of Grace* (2012, Mercer University Press) and/

or his thirty-plus works. Others will gain deeper insights from this new publication.

Yet, many of us have had the pleasure through the years of sitting in his classes, hosting him in our churches, and participating in stimulating personal discussions. The chapters that follow are more indication of his knowledge and his remarkable ability to synthesize and present with understanding and inspiration.

Enjoy his writing and insights. Immerse yourself into his teachings. Discover afresh and anew the traditions and disciplines of our faith. Sit with these words; be silent in the midst of your thoughts. Let the Spirit impact you and lead you to impact others. While you won't experience the depth of those days in October, you will be moved as you read and contemplate what the Spirit is saying to you in these pages.

The church is richer because of the gifts of Glenn Hinson. My ministry is richer because of his friendship and teaching. Our hope is that through these chapters your ministry and life will also be enriched. These lectures are another remarkable gift from a hero of our faith. Yet, in true Hinson form, he doesn't take the form of a "caped crusader" or "ancient demi-god." Rather, he enters our lives with a quiet humility, offering profound insights that will inform us while transforming us. . . . Sounds like a hero to me.

Bo Prosser, Ed. D.
Coordinator for Missional Congregations
Cooperative Baptist Fellowship
Atlanta, Ga.
2012

Acknowledgments

T his book is the distillation of many years of reflection on the spirituality of Baptists within the context of Christian spirituality as it has developed through the ages. Because I have had occasion to give lectures and to write articles on various aspects of this issue, I have drawn some of the book's content from previously published materials.

Some elements in Part 1, for instance, overlap an essay on "Everyday Spirituality for Ordinary Time" that I wrote for *Interpretation*, a journal published by the faculty of Union Theological Seminary in Richmond, Virginia. Part 2 is a slightly revised and updated essay published in *Protestant Spiritual Traditions*, edited by Frank C. Senn (Mahwah, NJ: Paulist Press, 1986). Parts 3 and 4 are significantly expanded versions of "Baptist Approaches to Spirituality" published in the Spring 2002 issue of *Baptist History & Heritage*. In Part 5 you will hear echoes of "Church as Schola Caritatis" that appeared in *Weavings* XXVI (pp. 40-47).

Some ideas, especially those about contemplation in a world of action, have ties to *A Serious Call to a Contemplative Lifestyle*, first published in 1974. Taken as a whole, however, this is my first effort to put together my most carefully considered thoughts about Baptist spirituality past, present, and future.

I thank Hal Melton, associate pastor of Trinity Baptist Church in Raleigh, North Carolina, and Johnny Sears, director of the Academy for Spiritual Formation, Board of Discipleship of the United Methodist Church in Nashville, Tennessee, for inviting me to give this series of lectures in a 5-Day Academy for Spiritual Formation sponsored jointly by the Cooperative Baptist Fellowship (CBF) and the Upper Room at Saint

Ignatius Center in Atlanta, October 14-19, 2012. I thank all of the participants for intense listening and for asking discerning questions that helped both to confirm and to reshape my thinking.

I am grateful to Blake Kendrick, associate pastor of First Baptist Church in Greenwood, South Carolina, for suggesting that I publish the series of articles. Finally, I thank John Pierce, editor of *Baptists Today*, who quickly outlined two or three options, one of which was publication of the series as a book.

Introduction

The central thesis of this book is that Baptists should recover the contemplative tradition with which they began in the early seventeenth century and teach others how to live contemplatively in an age and culture far removed from contemplation. Through our four centuries, especially in America, cultural experience has reshaped and is reshaping our spirituality and worship in ways whereby God ends up as the one we expect to serve our programs and whims rather than the one we serve.

I must give Thomas Merton credit for my basic thesis. Just a week or two after I took my first group of church history students to the Abbey of Gethsemani on November 7, 1960, he sent me a packet of manuals he put together to teach monastic novices. I thumbed through them, but I had no idea how they might relate to what I was doing in training Baptist ministers. To be quite honest, my perusal of them gave me only a glimmer of insight into the importance of tradition in forming people in the spiritual life.

Like most Baptists, I had great suspicion of tradition as "the dead hand of the past." Not until I read all of Merton's writings after his untimely death on December 10, 1968, did I begin to grasp why in his manuals Merton sought, more than anything else, to expose those who sat at his feet to the teachings of the saints all through Christian history, first in the scriptures and then in other writings.

I've learned a great deal from Thomas Merton about the life of the spirit in the world of today, especially about contemplation in a world of action. No insight, however, surpasses in importance a distinction he made between tradition and convention. Convention, he contended, is the husk, the external that we can discard. It is the non-essential. Tradition is the kernel, the essence that we cannot do without. With that distinction I began to understand more clearly why the Apostle Paul spoke about "handing on" the tradition he also had received, for example, about the resurrection (1 Cor. 15:3). It was vital tradition.

Early in my teaching career as my contacts with other Christians expanded, I went through a period when I found little in the Baptist tradition that measured up to what I found in other traditions. Baptist worship, for instance, seemed trite and superficial alongside the rich liturgy of the Anglican or Episcopal Church. Baptist spirituality could not compare with the priceless cornucopia of Roman Catholicism. A writing assignment brought me up short. "Some in-depth research into the spirituality of my Puritan ancestors opened my eyes to riches I had never discerned before, some of which equaled the finest treasures in all Christian history. Over [several] centuries Baptists had let many of these gems lose their luster, but a little polishing and cleaning showed that, even now, treasures are latent in the Baptist treasury, awaiting recovery."[1]

In this small volume I will look first at what I call the crisis of Baptist spirituality posed by our current lifestyle and ask how well prepared we are to meet the challenge. From there I will take you back to Baptist/Puritan beginnings as contemplatives engaged in a quest for heart religion manifested in transformed lives and social concern, remarkably close to the goal of contemplatives through the centuries. Next we will look at the reshaping of Baptist spirituality as a consequence of the Great Awakening and the frontier revivals and of the impact of the burgeoning business model on Baptist spirituality. In the final chapter I will try to project a vision for Baptist spirituality today. Above all, we Baptists should seek to make our churches schools of love that will offer to the world something it doesn't already have more of than it needs.

Notes

[1] "Reassessing the Puritan Heritage in Worship/Spirituality: A Search for a Method," *Worship*, 53 (July 1979), 319.

Part 1

The Crisis of Baptist Spirituality
God the Forgotten One

The word "crisis" may sound a bit alarmist, and I have probably chosen it for that reason. I recognize that some may not see any cause for alarm. Baptists have been like they are for more than 400 years, so why suggest that what is happening today in Baptist spirituality is of critical importance? We will keep plugging ahead for another 400 years just as we have done the last 400.

I sometimes feel a little cynical myself and shrug off the "holy nudge" to say a prophetic word that might get Baptists, this people with whom I've enjoyed a love/hate relationship through most of my eighty years, to act more faithfully as God's people. In spirituality, though, Baptists have changed a lot in these four centuries. They have evolved from the contemplative approach they inherited from their medieval forbears to a pragmatic one in which God is the forgotten one. They have become more interested in telling God what to do than in listening to what God is telling them.

Attentiveness to God is, I think, what spirituality is all about. It is the bottom line. To define the "crisis" in Baptist spirituality today, or Christian spirituality in general, I would say that inattentiveness to God is the same fault believers have suffered from since the first humans emerged on earth, but now it is magnified in the culture we have been creating for ourselves. It is the magnification that raises our situation to crisis level.

Busyness

Most of you will know that for many years I've harped on two facets of this problem: our busyness and our distractedness. We live in a culture that likes to put us on a treadmill of activity for activity's sake and, as Thomas Kelly said long ago, creates "absurdly crowded calendars of appointments through which so many pantingly and frantically gasp."[1]

If we are honest with ourselves, however, I think we can recognize that this stems less from what our culture imposes than from what our egos require. Activity makes us feel needed and wanted. Meaningful activity, most assuredly, is important to our self-esteem. Long-term unemployed persons, those who have just been fired, or even those who have retired voluntarily from a job may hit rock bottom.

The semester after I retired from Baptist Theological Seminary at Richmond in 1999, I experienced depression. That surprised me because I'm usually an upbeat person. That semester, however, watching a news account or reading a sad story would bring tears. Fortunately, before the semester ended I had calls to teach at Lexington Theological Seminary and Louisville Presbyterian Seminary. Job offers saved me!

Meaningful activity is very important to self-esteem. I underscore the word "meaningful"—not just activity, but activity that matters boosts our self-images.

In our culture, however, not only activity but also quantity of activity determines how we feel about ourselves. Ninety-nine times out of a hundred, if you ask someone, "How are you?" you will get a litany of activities. "Oh, I'm so busy. I'm working two jobs. I am on three committees at church; I chair one of them. I belong to two book clubs. I'm involved in volunteer work with the Volunteers of America, Goodwill, and the Red Cross." By the time she finishes the list, you feel worn out and look around for a chair to sit in for a while. Gather with a group of ministers or professors, and you may hear something similar.

At Southern Seminary we used to meet for coffee in the faculty lounge. We would get out our appointment books. I would glance out of the corner of one eye at a colleague's appointment book and notice that he had three more engagements this month than I had, and, whimpering inwardly, I would shrink back into myself like a puppy that had just wet on the kitchen floor. "Some churches needed *him* more than they needed *me*." Or I might notice out of the corner of my other eye that I had two more engagements this week than that colleague. Ahem! I would recover some modicum of self-esteem.

Distractedness

Both external and internal pressures, therefore, work together to increase busyness, one of the major reasons for diminishment of attention to God. *Distractedness* exacerbates busyness. For many years we have worried about noise pollution. Thankfully my children have taken much greater care than I did to protect their hearing by using earplugs or gadgets that reduce noise of motors or other devices. When I participated in an ROTC summer camp at Fort Bliss, Texas, in 1953, trainers in artillery batteries merely encouraged us to put our hands over our ears when the guns fired. When you were the gunner, you found even that difficult. Today, troops wear high-tech earphones to protect themselves around the noisemakers. In retrospect, I think that is where the deterioration of my hearing began. Noise diminishes sensitivity to sound. Loud noises over a long period can deafen. When you go into a basketball arena or a baseball stadium where sound level rockets up above 130 decibels, how well can you hear when you exit?

In recent years Americans have had to pay attention to the distractions caused by the use of cell phones, particularly while driving. You have probably experienced much the same "cuss-inducing" frustration I have felt when the light changed and the driver two cars ahead carried on a conversation with someone or texted on her phone. But worse happens.

About a third of fatal automobile accidents last year resulted either from talking or texting while driving. Kentuckians got a particularly vivid reminder of the price of distractedness in 2010 when the driver of a huge semi truck yakking on his cell phone let his rig roar across the median on I-65 near Horse Cave and smash into a van carrying an Amish family to a wedding. A moment's distraction wiped out eleven lives. The Kentucky legislature banned texting, but not talking on cell phones. Many states have legislation under consideration that would ban both texting and cell phone usage while driving.

More recently we have begun to speak about *light* pollution. It, too, distracts us. When I taught at Baptist Theological Seminary at Richmond, on nighttime trips down the Blue Ridge Parkway I often pulled off in one of the many sidings, turned off the headlights of the car, and got out to look up into the night sky. Would you believe, I could see jillions of stars? I had almost forgotten they were there. Lights of the city virtually blotted them out entirely.

Through the centuries *homo sapiens* have found ways to cope with the diminishment of attentiveness to God by these pollutions. They have retreated, drawn back, to escape from the press and struggle of everyday existence. They have spent time in solitude and silence. Solitude gives room for the senses to recover their homing instinct. As noise and over-exposure to light desensitize, so solitude and silence resensitize. Sadly, the more dependent our culture becomes on the pseudo-nature of technology, the less it permits or encourages us to take time for solitude and silence in nature that might allow our sensors to recover from the bombardment they endure day after day and hour after hour.

The Shallowing

There is no question that busyness and distractedness pose massive challenges for spirituality in today's world. There is something more subtle and sinister, however, that has intruded recently—a phenomenon that people of my generation did not confront as it is now impacting the current generation of seekers after mature faith. You and I are participants in a massive revolution in the way we humans appropriate and transmit knowledge and relate to the world around us. This revolution in many ways reverses the one that took place at the end of the fifteenth and beginning of the sixteenth centuries as a result of a great technological revolution: Gutenberg's invention of movable type.

Whereas in the Middle Ages people relied on images and touch, humanists and Protestant reformers placed more confidence in the written and spoken word—scripture and sermon. They translated scriptures into the vernacular and put them into the hands of ordinary people. They preached long and thorough sermons. They wrote book after book after book. Due to our current cybernetic revolution, you and I are seeing this trend reversed. Whereas my generation relied on the typographic approach, my grandson's generation is becoming increasingly dependent on an iconic and visual approach necessitated by computers.

Let me affirm heartily that this revolution has produced rich benefits, and I feel badly handicapped that I came along too early and am now too old to take full advantage of them. Until 1992 when I went to Richmond to teach at Baptist Theological Seminary at Richmond, I typed all of my articles and books on a 1923 Underwood Standard. A pool of expert typists used computers to put them in finished and nearly inerrant form. But the fledgling seminary I moved to in Richmond had no secretarial pool to do my finished typing. Instead, Tom Halbrooks, the dean, outfitted me with a beginner's computer and said, "You are now your typing pool." Thus was I dragged kicking and screaming into the cybernetic age.

Despite natural resistance to change, I soon became thankful for the countless ways in which the computer had eased my toil, enhanced my ability to produce articles and books, and brought the world to my doorstep. What has happened is awesome! I sat with mouth agape before my iMac last year, for instance, when we "Skyped" with Elizabeth (my daughter), Lee, Garrison, and Emme living in Hungary during Elizabeth's sabbatical. IMing with friends in Australia—the opposite side of our planet—overwhelms this octogenarian who, as a child, was agog to hear radio programs piped from Del Rio, Texas, all the way to the Missouri Ozarks. What is happening is incredible, fabulous, mind-boggling!

More fabulous still, all of this has come along at a time when my deafness has reached the point where I could scarcely trust my capacity for hearing at all. No sweat, though, thanks to the digital revolution, for my family and friends can e-mail me, and virtually all television programs come equipped with the possibility of both seeing and hearing the sounds.

Yet let me say that vast revolutions cost something. They bring advances, but those who participate in them had better count the cost. In this case the cost I want to talk about has to do with an impact the Internet is making on our spirituality, specifically on our attentiveness to God—what prayer is in essence. If we humans have always had trouble paying attention to God in the midst of busy and distracting lives, how will we do it at all when the Internet gets done altering our brains in such a way as to make it difficult for us to be attentive to a book or a paper or anything else for any length of time?

In his best-selling book *The Shallows: What the Internet Is Doing to Our Brains*, Nicholas Carr reported this disturbing news:

> Dozens of studies by psychologists, neurobiologists, educators, and Web designers point to the same conclusion: when we go online, we enter an environment that promotes cursory reading, hurried and distracted thinking, and superficial learning.[2]
>
> . . . With the exception of alphabets and numbers systems, the Net may well be the single most powerful mind-altering technology that has ever come into

general use. At the very least, it's the most powerful that has come along since the book.[3]

. . . It returns us to our native state of bottom-up distractedness, while presenting us with far more distractions than our ancestors ever had to contend with.[4]

Carr goes on to point out that the distractedness the Net encourages differs from intentional diversion of the mind to weigh a decision: "The Net's cacophony of stimuli short-circuits both conscious and unconscious thought, preventing our minds from thinking either deeply or creatively."[5]

A little cogitation will tell you where I am headed in this as it relates to spirituality. The ability to pay attention is precisely what is taking a severe beating from this new technology. In consequence, God ends up perched out there on the periphery of our consciousness, of no great importance in our busy lives.

I don't think I exaggerate when I say that it is not easy to learn how to pray or to keep at it when we have learned how. Teresa of Avilá, the first woman named a "Doctor of the Church" in the main because of her contribution to Christian understanding of prayer, confessed that she spent twenty years learning how.[6] Admittedly, she didn't get serious in her effort to learn until a three-year illness and a near-death experience put some pressure on. She discovered what everyone who takes prayer seriously will discover: Prayer is, above all, response to the prior love of God. As Bernard of Clairvaux reminded his fellow monks, ". . . every soul among you that is seeking God should know that it has been anticipated by [God], and has been sought by [God] before it began to seek [God]."[7]

It couldn't happen any other way, could it? How could we mortals get God's attention, the attention of the God of a universe of 150-plus billion galaxies. We can't yell loud enough, build a Babel tower high enough, or send a space ship far enough to get God's attention unless God has chosen to enter into our consciousness. If we pray, then, we have to learn how to respond. We have to cultivate this attentiveness.

If Nicholas Carr is right, however, that is precisely where the Internet is tripping us up. Google, on which most of us rely heavily, epitomizes the problem. "Google's profits," Carr charged, "are tied directly to the velocity of people's information intake."[8] It therefore makes every effort to disrupt our attention. "Google is, quite literally, in the business of distraction."[9] Add MySpace, Facebook, and Twitter, and we can only expect acceleration of information delivery. Google wants to digitize every book and make it available Online. Quite clearly, we have to acknowledge the benefit of efficient collection of data, but it poses a problem for us in that it does not leave room for meditation or contemplation. "Mentally, we're in perpetual locomotion," says Carr.[10] He remarked later:

> In Google's world, which is the world we enter when we go online, there's little place for the pensive stillness of deep reading or the fuzzy indirection of contemplation. Ambiguity is not an opening for insight but a bug to be fixed. The human brain is just an outdated computer that needs a faster processor and a bigger hard drive—and better algorithms to steer the course of its thought.[11]

You can see here perhaps why I speak about a "crisis" in spirituality today. Long before Google was born, Thomas Merton put his finger squarely on the problem modern technological development has created for humankind and that the Internet now magnifies. Humans, he argued, possess "an instinctive need for harmony and peace, for tranquility, order and meaning,"[12] but western technological society denies them these things. It leaves no space for contemplation; yet contemplation is essential to meaningful action. According to Merton,

> He who attempts to act and do things for others or for the world without deepening his own self-understanding, freedom, integrity and capacity to love, will not have anything to give others. He will communicate to them nothing but the contagion of his own obsessions, his aggressiveness, his ego-centered ambitions, his delusions about ends and means, his doctrinaire prejudices and ideas.[13]

Insofar as I can see, the Internet is no friend of contemplation. It is doing something to our brains that will affect our spiritual lives from this day forward unless we deliberately attempt to counter its effects. The question we must now ask is whether Baptists are doing anything that deepens self-understanding, freedom, integrity, and capacity to love and thence to act and do things for others in a culture increasingly intent on dissipating our capacity for mindfulness of God.

Baptist Spirituality Confronting the Crisis

As I begin this reflection, I am sensitive to the fact that one group of Christians, which includes a big bunch of Baptists, feels uncomfortable with the whole idea of spirituality. The concept and the practice of it are too subjective. The idea of attentiveness to God is too subjective. We can't control it; and for this group, control is critical.

The theologian Karl Barth thought that about prayer. When Douglas Steere met him in a Benedictine monastery in Germany in 1933, he asked Barth why, if he thought prayer too subjective, he came to a place where its inhabitants spend all their time in prayer. Barth replied, "To refute them." Thankfully, Barth changed his mind.[14] But some Christian fundamentalists or evangelicals have not. They insist on more objective religion, and they find it in an inerrant Bible and creeds. Just believe the Bible; that settles it.

The problem I see in this attitude is that the Bible insists on something very different. It points us to God. It directs us to ask, seek, and knock. It urges us to seek first God's mysterious presence and God's affirming of us. It speaks about the Spirit of God who directs us not only to act, but also to act in ways pleasing to God. In the pages that follow, therefore, I will be addressing people, specifically Baptists, who want to develop a more intimate relationship with God and not those content to let the Bible take the place of God in their lives. Admittedly, you can't control God who is beyond human comprehension, but a god you can control can't help anybody.

I'm a little uncertain how best to frame the question with which we need to wrestle here. Perhaps I can state it in this way: What is there about Baptists and their heritage that will make it difficult for them to live authentically God-conscious lives in a culture that confronts them deliberately with the busyness, distractedness, and shallowing that ours does? Permit me to enumerate some of the most glaring features.

Failure to Listen

Baptists are a talkative bunch, and talkers usually aren't good listeners. Like our Puritan forbears, we bought fully and unhesitatingly into the typographic revolution that occurred on the cusp of the Reformation of the sixteenth century. We closed monasteries. We replaced the stained glass windows, statuaries, mosaics, and elaborate use of symbols recounting the story of salvation with scripture reading and sermon.

In my earlier years, Baptist churches uniformly headed their bulletins "Preaching Service" and not "Worship Service." "Worship" had a sinister connotation, "liturgy" a catholic odor, so we could not use them, much less practice what they suggested. Prayer was by definition petition or intercession. As a matter of fact, in his classic work on prayer, Friedrich Heiler, a convert from Roman Catholicism to Lutheranism, argued that the only truly authentic prayer is the spontaneous type Luther prayed, and he negated out of hand the contemplative tradition followed by monks through the centuries, which had at one time nurtured Luther.[15]

Running in the typographic rut, I think we can see, puts us in a vulnerable position with reference to what has happened in the cybernetic revolution. Church members no longer sit still through hour-long sermons (or three-hour in the case of early Puritans). On the downside of this, as Neil Postman pointed out in *Amusing Ourselves to Death*, they demand entertainment. They want church to be like the programs they see on television. More seriously, they seek something words simply cannot satisfy, something that feeds them both visually and orally. Since television and the Internet have shortened their attention spans, however, they demand what you try to provide in concentrated form—sound bites and sight flashes, if you please.

Wordy Baptists have had trouble with silence that might enhance attentiveness to God. At Deer Park Baptist Church during the 1960s the pastor, Carman Sharp, tried to introduce some periods of silence into the Wednesday night prayer meeting. He started with one-minute silences. Ten or fifteen seconds after the silence began, you could hear throats being cleared, pages of Bibles and hymnals thrupping, feet scuffling on the carpet, and rear ends scooting on the pews. Things improved later, but I thought then: "God will have a heck of a time getting a word in edgewise among Baptists."

Missions and Evangelism

Baptists in America, especially the heirs of the Separate Baptists of the Great Awakening who migrated southwards, have a mania for missions and evangelism so intense that God plays second fiddle to the great cause. I mean no disrespect to people trying to fulfill the Great Commission, but obsession with discharging this obligation has resulted in a subtle shift from attention to God to the front end of the conversion process. Get them down the aisle to make a "decision." The invitation has become in some Baptist churches the main sacrament.

I was shocked years ago when I attended Kings Highway Baptist Church in St. Louis one Sunday morning to witness a young mother virtually drag twin four-year-olds down the aisle at the invitation. I don't think either child responded voluntarily or knew what was happening. More shocking still, the pastor took both children to the baptistery and baptized them that morning! Southern Baptist churches each year baptize hundreds of children in Sunday school primaries—ages three to five.

Obsession with Success

Closely connected to this issue, the business model has imposed itself on Baptists in America, and Baptists have bought into the success motif of the corporate world. That was bound to happen to the Southern Baptist Convention because it grew up with American business—first the railroads and then other dominant enterprises.

I suppose you can find worthy motives in both the corporate world and in the church, but you may also find a ruthless pragmatism connected with success as the chief criterion by which institutions measure what they do. We negotiate in order to achieve the objectives of the corporation. In the church that means we even negotiate with God rather than ask what God wants. I have the feeling that once Baptists come up with a program designed to do what a church wants, God had better get out of the way and let free enterprise work.

Insistence on Voluntary Religion

One of our most cherished Baptist tenets may also work against us here, specifically, the voluntary principle in religion. "To be authentic and responsible, faith must be free," we have insisted, "for God alone is Lord of the conscience." I'm not at all prepared to back away from our Baptist tenets, but we need to recognize that they tilt us toward individualism within a country in which such individualism goes to extremes. In our church life we have strongly resisted tradition and espoused an "I'll do as I please" mentality.

Hostility to tradition is very pronounced in Baptist life. My training in New Testament studies at Southern Seminary during the 1950s underscored skepticism toward any evidence found in tradition. An older colleague once told me that Hersey Davis, A. T. Roberson's successor in New Testament at Southern, pronounced the word "tradi . . . shun" in the most nasal way he could do it—like a stench in the nostrils.

Cecil Sherman, key leader in the forming of the Cooperative Baptist Fellowship, showed much the same attitude.

Baptists rely on the Bible alone. If you have the Bible, you don't need what happened in the centuries after the apostles. I am thankful that Thomas Merton helped me to see a distinction between "tradition" and "convention." Tradition is the essence, the kernel. Convention is the external, the husk. We can dispense with a lot of convention, but we must not discard tradition. The Greek word for tradition, *paradosis*, appears often in a positive sense in Paul's writings.

The "do as I please" mentality goes hand in hand with antipathy to tradition. Any Baptist, no matter how poorly educated, some would argue, can interpret the scripture as well as the most learned scholar because the Holy Spirit will inspire and guide us just as the Holy Spirit inspired and guided the persons who wrote the Bible. There is truth in that, but Baptists have carried it too far on many occasions.

From the beginning of our history in the seventeenth century we Baptists have harbored a strong suspicion of scholars. The earliest Baptists liked to say, "A degree from Oxford or Cambridge doth not a minister make." That attitude grew by leaps and bounds on the American frontier.

A former colleague once told me this anecdote: A student in a class taught by W. O. Carver stood up in class to avow his lack of learning. Vehemently, he said, "I thank God I'm ignorant. I thank God I'm ignoranter than a mule." Carver responded, "Young man, that prayer was answered before it was ever uttered." The long-term payoff of this attitude, however, can be seen in the displacement of scholars from Southern Baptist life in a populist movement called by inerrantists "the Baptist Reformation" or "conservative resurgence."

The Baptist antipathy to tradition and to authority has put Baptist spirituality at some risk in the current American setting where burgeoning religious pluralism is creating a veritable superstore of wares. Culture affects our choices more decisively than it does more structured churches because we don't have much to counterbalance it. Roman Catholic, Orthodox, and Anglican traditions provide their constituents with some guidance in the spiritual life through their more defined structures and teaching authorities. Baptists don't have such structures and delineated teaching authorities. In consequence, we are ripe candidates to be led off in all directions to sample a supermarket of religious wares with no solid criteria to evaluate them.

Conclusion

Wordiness, evangelistic excess, business mentality, and hyper-individualism generate an overload for a spirituality that must cope with busyness, distractedness, and shallowing in American culture today. Where shall we look for help? Among the many wares offered by our pluralistic society promising to satisfy our every need?

Richard Foster has listed a half dozen: contemplative, holiness, charismatic, social justice, evangelical, and incarnational. To these I would add: "secular, oriental or quasi-oriental, New Age, plus the prevailing spirituality of various religious bodies (Orthodox, Reformed, Methodist, etc.) and Roman Catholic religious orders (Ignatian, Carmelite, Franciscan, Dominican, etc.)."[16]

The question here is: How do we sort out which of these may help us the most? We have the same quandary that confronts my grandchildren when their parents take them into Toys "R" Us—overchoice. I think our way forward is to go back to discover what Christians have learned through the centuries.

Notes

[1] Thomas R. Kelly, *A Testament of Devotion* (New York: Harper & Row, 1941), 74.

[2] Nicholas Carr, *The Shallowing: What the Internet Is Doing to Our Brains* (New York and London: W. W. Norton & Co, 2011), 115–16. Italics mine.

[3] Ibid., 116.

[4] Ibid., 118. Italics mine.

[5] Ibid., 119.

[6] Teresa of Ávila, *The Autobiography of St. Teresa of Avilá*, translated by E. Allison Peers (Garden City, NY: Doubleday Image Books, 1960), 108.

[7] Bernard of Clairvaux, *Sermon 84 on the Song of Songs*, 2; Library of Christian Classics, XIII, Ray C. Petry, ed. (Philadelphia: Westminster Press, 1957), 74-75.

[8] Carr, *The Shallowing*, 156.

[9] Ibid., 157.

[10] Ibid., 168.

[11] Ibid., 173. Italics mine.

[12] Thomas Merton, *Faith and Violence* (Notre Dame, IN: University of Notre Dame, 1968), 215.

[13] Thomas Merton, *Contemplation in a World of Action* (Garden City, NJ: Doubleday & Co, 1971), 164.

[14] See Karl Barth, *Prayer*, ed. Don E. Saliers from the translation of Sara F. Terrien, 2nd ed. (Philadelphia: Westminster Press, 1972).

[15] See especially Friedrich Heiler, *Prayer: A Study in the History and Psychology of Prayer* (New York: Oxford University Press, 1932), 353-363.

[16] E. Glenn Hinson, "Trends in Baptist Spirituality," *Christian Spirituality Bulletin* 7 (Fall/Winter 1999), 3.

Part 2

Puritan/Baptist Spirituality
Survival of the Contemplative Tradition

To respond intelligently to the crisis we face in spirituality, we need to examine the path that led us here. For Baptists this entails our beginnings out of English Puritanism with an added touch of continental Anabaptism. At the outset in the seventeenth century, Baptists differed from other Puritans chiefly in their practice of believer's baptism, not adopting immersion as their mode of baptism until 1640. The major group of Baptists shaped their spirituality around John Calvin's theology just as other Puritans did. Hence, in this section I will begin with a depiction of Puritan/Baptist spirituality, sharing an essay I wrote around 1985 for *Protestant Spiritual Traditions*.[1]

Puritanism was spirituality. Puritans were to Protestantism what contemplatives and ascetics were to the medieval church. They parted company with their medieval forebears chiefly in the locus of their efforts. Where monks sought sainthood in monasteries, Puritans sought it everywhere—in homes, schools, town halls, and shops as well as churches. Sometimes knowingly, at other times unknowingly, they employed virtually the same methods monks used to obtain the same goal: "the saints' rest," heaven, or "full and glorious enjoyment of God." Like the monks, Puritans were zealous of heart religion manifested in transformation of life and manners. Impatient with halfway commitments, they kindled fires for unreserved, enthusiastic embracing of the covenant. Everything they did, they did with solemnity and determination.

The essence of piety, declared Lewis Bayly, bishop of Bangor, in *The Practise of Pietie*, a work first published in 1610 that shaped the mold of Puritan spirituality, is "to joyne together, in watching, fasting, praying, reading the Scriptures, keeping his Sabboths, hearing Sermons, receiving the holy Communion, relieving the Poore, exercising in all humilitie the workes of Pietie to God, and walking conscionably in the duties of our calling towards men."[2] In those words he summed up the whole Puritan platform.

The Goal of Puritan Spirituality

The Puritan vision included both this world and the next. Ultimately, Puritans played out their own version of *contemptus mundi*. Avid students of Hebrews, they "looked forward to the city which has foundations, whose builder and maker is God" (Heb. 11:10); they journeyed to a "better country, that is, a heavenly one" (11:16). They were pilgrims on the way to "Mount Zion, the heavenly Jerusalem, the innumerable company of angels, and the spirits of just people made perfect" (12:22, 24), the paradise of God in which dwelled the patriarchs, the prophets, the saints, the angels, and Christ himself. Or, Revelation-like, they dreamed of a city that "shone like the sun" with gold-paved streets where the inhabitants continually praised God and where neither night nor suffering nor sorrow ever entered.[3]

It is not surprising that Puritans had a near-obsession about death and dying. Emerging in an age when infant mortality was high and the average life span less than age thirty, they integrated this preoccupation realistically into their whole Calvinist scheme of divine omnipotence, human wretchedness, and predestination. They feared death, and they wanted no one to forget that death brought punishment as well as reward. Those who did not fear had much to worry about. The saint should live as a dying person among dying persons.

At the same time the Puritans, like saints of other ages, viewed death as a release and a relief. For the elect, death opened the way to a life of unending bliss. Times of sickness and death could open one to the working of divine grace. In doubt and struggle lay assurance that one knew the saving grace of God, the all-important element in the whole pilgrimage.[4] In the Puritan scheme, death was the fearsome river that separated

Beulah Land from Mount Zion, the heavenly city itself. It was the most important stage on life's pilgrimage—infancy, youth, middle age, death, and after death. All life should prepare one for it.

Keen as was the Puritans' longing for heaven, however, their chief focus of attention was not on the other world but on this one. Following their mentor John Calvin, they rejected medieval monastic otherworldliness. So long as they lived in the "wilderness" that this world is, they would practice "the life of heaven" on earth. As Christopher Hill has pointed out in his insightful study of *Society and Puritanism in Pre-Revolutionary England*, Puritanism had to do with more than religious matters.

Puritans belonged to "the industrious sort of people," who stressed labor as a duty to one's neighbor, society, commonwealth, and humankind, and viewed idleness with horror. They denounced popish religion as the mother of ineptitude in trade, hard work, and accumulation of wealth. Monks, nuns, and mendicants, they charged, lived in idleness and thus did not contribute to production. Unmarried clergy led to a declining population. Superstition permitted extravagance in adornment of churches. Too many holidays were detrimental to production. Friars lived on alms of the poor and thus inhibited their rise above poverty.[5]

In their quest for "a new Reformation" that would surpass the "half-Reformation" of 1517,[6] Puritans emphasized the family as the basic unit of society. By reducing the authority of the clergy, the Reformation of the sixteenth century had simultaneously elevated the role of heads of households. Henry VIII, Edward VI, and Elizabeth all directed family heads "to have especial regard to the good government and ordering of the same."[7] Not surprisingly, therefore, Puritans emphasized still more vigorously the piety of the family.

Arthur Dent printed family prayers in *The Plaine Man's Pathway to Heaven*, Lewis Bayly in *The Practise of Pietie*. "The family farm or workshop played in the world of early capitalism the part that the great noble household or monastery had played in medieval society," Christopher Hill observed.[8] Heads of families took charge of both the physical and the spiritual welfare of those under them. "Parents and masters of families are in God's stead to their children and servants," J. Mayne said in his explanation of the English catechism.[9]

The Way to the Goal

Passing through "this world of sin" on the way to the heavenly Jerusalem, Puritans revived and adapted a regimen of self-examination and prayer that monks had employed for centuries. Thoroughly Augustinian, like their mentor John Calvin, they emphasized human sinfulness and divine grace. Christians, Richard Baxter declared, should "make it the great labor of their lives to grow in grace, to strengthen and advance the interest of Christ in their souls, and to weaken and subdue the interest of the flesh."[10] Grace alone could bring one to faith and repentance for sin and guide one in the way of salvation. It alone could soften the heart and energize the mind. Accordingly, the perpetual Puritan prayer went something like Cotton Mather's: "Lord, help mee now unto the Redeeming of time, and the Spending of as much as I can, of it, in a perpetual Exercise of Grace!"[11]

Prerequisite to the pilgrimage, the favorite Puritan metaphors for the Christian life, were election by God in the Son, being "born again," discovery of "a deep sense of divine things," an awareness of a change of will, entrance into covenant with Christ, and perseverance in this covenant to the end.[12] Puritans unquestioningly accepted Calvin's predestinarian views. God is absolutely sovereign. Not a sparrow falls to the ground save by his design and decree. By his inscrutable will, God has decreed that some would be saved and some lost. It behooves all, but especially the "elect," to inquire continually into the security of their "election." The important thing, Baxter and most Puritans would say, is "whether such or such a saving grace be in thee in sincerity or not."[13] Self-examination of this sort could and did lead to serious problems, since the Puritans made no special provision for spiritual direction that could mitigate the harsh and capricious aspects of self-criticism.

John Bunyan, for instance, plunged into severe depression using the Puritan method. Relying on scriptures darting into his mind at random to tell him whether he belonged to the elect, he would sometimes hear a word of assurance and at other times one of judgment, especially from the passage in Hebrews about Esau selling his birthright. His moods went up; they went down. He feared he had committed the unpardonable sin. He reached the point of suicide. Little by little, a word of grace, which a spiritual guide might have spoken to him long before, broke through: in reading the preface to Luther's commentary on Galatians, in overhearing the conversation of some women at Bedford about a "new birth," in counsels of Bedford pastor John Gifford and in "My grace is sufficient for thee"

(2 Cor. 12:9) as he sat meditating in the Bedford congregation of which he later became pastor. Still tormented, he prayed that the Esau passage and the sufficiency passage might meet and do battle in his mind at the same time. They did and, fortunately, the sufficiency passage won.[14]

However much everything depended on election, the "one great qualification" from a human standpoint, according to Baxter, was being "born again" (John 3:3)—conversion of heart, mind, and will. Conversion was the Spirit's work, requiring little if any human assistance. Early in the Puritan era, which was riding a wave of revival both in England and in New England, not much coaxing was required. Multitudes were engaging in the most rigorous soul-searching. A generation or two later, however, religious fervor dampened, and as it did some perceived an appropriate role for "means" to effect conversions. In the "Great Awakening" (1720-1760), Puritans split over the place of "religious affections" in conversion, some favoring and some opposing the use of means.

In the Calvinist scheme, conversion was only the beginning of the pilgrimage. After and not before it came conviction of sin and redirection of the will toward God. Then one could enter into the covenant with God through Christ in which one must persevere to the end. The covenant stood at the center of Puritan thought and life. "We Covenant with the Lord and one with an other," the Salem Covenant of 1629 read, "and doe bynd our selves in the presence of God, to walke together in all his waies, according as he is pleased to reveale himself unto us in his Blessed word of truth."[15] Seven years later, the Puritans spelled out particulars. Salvation lay in keeping the covenant by grace, but to most it must have seemed like living under the law again.

Though the long-range goal was heaven, therefore, the immediate task of the Puritan was to live a heavenly life on earth. Yet Puritans were well aware of obstacles on the way. Lewis Bayly listed misunderstanding of scriptures, the evil example of noted persons, prosperity, presumption of God's mercy, evil company, fear lest piety make one too sad or pensive, and the hope of long life.[16] Efforts to steer around such hindrances did much to create the Puritan ethos so often caricatured in modern thought. Where Puritanism lapsed into externalism, however, it did so unintentionally. Puritans coveted anything but "mere preparatives for the heavenly life, without any acquaintance with the thing itself."[17] They wanted authentic, sincere, soulful commitment that would overflow into every dimension of thought and activity.

The Puritans relied on a host of traditional techniques taken mostly from the ascetic and contemplative tradition, their critique of monasticism notwithstanding. We cannot assume any uniformity among these nonconformists, of course, but devout Puritans would have employed many of the same devotional exercises.

A practice expected of everyone was reading or, perhaps one should say, praying and poring over the scriptures in search of the Word of God. Puritans—Baptists included—were "people of the Book." Thus when Christian, in *The Pilgrim's Progress*, left his "roll" behind inadvertently, he had to return for it, for it was "the assurance of his life, and acceptance of the desired haven."[18]

Lewis Bayly directed the devout to read a chapter morning, noon, and night so as to read through the entire Bible in a year, then to meditate on its exhortations and counsels to good works and a holy life, threatenings of judgment for sins, blessings, God's promises for Christian virtues (patience, chastity, mercy, almsgiving, zeal in his service, charity, faith, and trust in God), and God's gracious deliverance and special blessings. These chapters, he insisted, should not be read as history but as letters sent directly from God, and therefore be read with reverence as if God stood by and spoke the words directly to the reader, thus inciting one to virtue and repentance of sin.[19] Cotton Mather developed what he called "porismatic" reading that entailed reading "with such devout Attention, as to fetch at least one *Observation*, and one *Supplication*, a *Note* and a *Wish* out of every *Verse* in all the Bible."[20]

Puritans were a highly literate people, turning out vast amounts of devotional material. The devout kept daily logs of both their inner perceptions and their outward activities in diaries and journals. They wrote biographies, autobiographies, and pious fiction modeling the pilgrimage. They did searching critiques of contemporary society.[21]

The heart of Puritan, as of monastic, devotion was prayer and meditation. To be true prayer, it had to come from the heart. Prayer, John Bunyan insisted, "is a sincere, sensible, affectionate pouring out of the heart or soul to God through Christ, in the strength and assistance of the holy Spirit, for such things as God hath promised, or, according to the Word, for the good of the Church, with submission, in Faith, to the Will of God."[22]

Not all Puritans would have gone to the extreme Bunyan did in rejecting all forms of prayer, even the Lord's Prayer, as a hindrance to the Spirit. Some wrote commentaries on the latter. But they would have agreed with Bunyan in emphasizing the heart. A test frequently applied to commitment was the disposition of the heart in prayer for mercy. And Puritans could report experiences worthy of a Bernard of Clairvaux or a Teresa of Avilá. Cotton Mather, for instance, spoke of his heart being "rapt into those heavenly Frames, which would have turned a Dungeon into a Paradise" or "raised unto Raptures almost Insupportable, when I was Expressing my Love to God, and Beleeving His Love to me, . . ."[23]

Puritans knew, too, the power of tears—"compunction," the monks called it—as a conditioner of the heart for prayer. A youthful Cotton Mather had the habit of prostrating himself on the floor and pouring out tears concerning his "wickedness" as "the most filthy Sinner out of Hell."[24] On another occasion, emptying his heart in confession, he "melted into a flood of Tears."[25]

Puritans emphasized both public and private confession as a remedy for sin. Calvin, of course, included confession and absolution in the liturgy of Geneva. His heirs followed in his footsteps. A substantial part of the Puritan formation process, however, revolved around examination of one's conscience as a sinner in a manner much like that of Ignatius Loyola. If sickness struck, one should inquire into sin, for in the Puritan view illness almost certainly indicated divine disfavor and need of repentance. And "where sin abounded, grace super-abounded" (Rom. 5:15), especially to those who confessed. "A Stream of Tears gushed out of my Eyes, upon my Floor," Cotton Mather testified, "while I had my Soul inexpressibly irradiated with Assurances, of especially two or three Things, bore in upon me."[26]

Another conditioner that figured prominently in the Puritan regimen, both publicly and privately, was fasting or "humiliation." In both Old and New England, officials called for fasts during times of crisis, convinced that the public welfare depended on the piety of the faithful. The General Court of Massachusetts, for instance, set July 7, 1681 as "a day of public Humiliation" on the grounds that the time required "greater fervency and frequency in the most solemn seekings of God in the face of Jesus Christ, than wee have ordinarily had experience of; . . ." The decree ticked off concern about Puritan woes in Great Britain and anti-Christian sentiment, a drought, and other awful circumstances in England. [27]

Fasts, whether public or private, aimed at the abasing of the sinner so as to soften the heart and get it in condition for divine direction and assurance. "Inexpressible Self-Abhorrence, for my abominable Sinfulness before the Holy Lord," wrote Cotton Mather of one "secret" fast, "was the Design, and the very Spirit of my Devotions this Day." By humbling himself, however, he "received a new, a strong, a wonderful Assurance from Heaven (melting mee into Tears of Joy!) that my Sins are all pardoned thro' the Blood of Christ, and that notwithstanding all my horrid Sinfulness, I shall be employ'd in great Services for His Name."[28]

Puritans knew they could take nothing for granted in their march toward Beulah Land. For persons adamant in their opposition to Roman Catholic works-righteousness or salvation by works, they spoke surprisingly often and emphatically of duties the covenant imposed upon them. For those who would maintain a heavenly walk, Richard Baxter prescribed conviction that heaven is one's only treasure, labor to know it as one's own and how near it is, frequent and serious talk about it, effort to raise one's affections nearer to it in every activity, "improvement of every object and event," much "evangelical work and praise," careful observing and cherishing of motions of the Spirit, and care for bodily health.[29] Their verbal gymnastics notwithstanding, these prescriptions differed not at all in any essential way from the program of medieval monks and nuns![30]

Early on, Puritans perfected methods of meditation and contemplation supportive of heart religion. According to the master guide of Puritan contemplation, Richard Baxter, contemplation should occur at stated times to avoid omission, frequently to prevent shyness between God and the soul and prevent unskillfulness and "loss of heat and life," and seasonably. Prayer should be engaged in several times daily, more frequently on the Sabbath, on special occasions when God warms the heart, when sick, and when dying.[31] Devout Puritans often spent entire days in prayer. They frequently threw up "ejaculatory" prayers as occasion demanded. Obviously the goal was to "pray without ceasing" (1 Thess. 5:17).

Puritans emphasized privacy in prayer and literally arranged "closets" for that purpose. One's covenant is an intimate matter requiring highly personal conversation. At the same time they made prayer a visible public concern in the family, church gatherings, especially on the Sabbath, and other settings. In public prayer, Puritans made much use of the Psalms. They peppered their prayers with scripture quotations, which was natural in view of their constant searching through the Bible.

Although Puritans would not have distinguished as precisely as the monks did between levels of prayer (*cogitatio, meditatio,* and *contemplatio*

of Hugo of St. Victor), they did differentiate meditation or contemplation from ordinary prayer, which is perhaps best characterized as "mental"
prayer. Given their strong accentuation of individual piety, we should not
be surprised to find much improvisation in prayer and meditation, but
the best specimens reveal remarkable likeness to medieval forms.

Contemplation, instructed Baxter, requires preparation of the heart
by freeing it of the world—business, troubles, joys—and by attaining
the greatest solemnity of heart and mind through apprehension of the
presence of God and God's incomprehensible greatness. Detachment,
Meister Eckhart would say. "The most powerful prayer . . . is that which
proceeds from an empty spirit."[32]

"Consideration," rational control of the whole process, is "the great
instrument by which this heavenly work is carried on," said Richard
Baxter. The Puritans knew that the heart is "where it's at," but they feared
the emotions and the imagination. Both could go wild. Consideration,
a concept used also by Loyola in the *Spiritual Exercises*, would establish a
proper direction in meditation. As Baxter described its effects, it "opens
the door between the head and the heart," "presents to the affections
those things which are most important," "reasons the case with a man's
[or woman's] own heart," "exalts reason to its just authority," "makes
reason strong and active," and "can continue and persevere in this rational employment."[33]

Capricious as they may be, nevertheless, in the Puritan view the affections count most in heart religion. Meditation has to do with affective
rather than cognitive capacities. And here is where imagination enters
in. To incite love, desire, hope, courage or boldness, and joy or their
opposites (hatred of sin, godly fear, godly shame and grief, unfeigned
repentance, self-indignation, jealously regarding one's heart, and pity for
those in danger of losing immortal salvation), Baxter urged use of biblical images, soliloquies, and "sensible objects," warning, however: "Don't,
like the papists, draw them (Moses, Jesus, or other biblical characters)
in pictures but get the liveliest picture of them in the mind that thou
possibly canst by contemplating the scripture account of them . . ."[34]
(A tall order, surely, for the "papist" Loyola, whose spirituality exerted
much influence on Catholic spirituality and insisted on mental images,
too.)[35] Biblical images would supposedly arouse the right emotions and
thus increase love or desire for God, hope, courage, etc.

Again like medieval contemplatives such as Bernard of Clairvaux, the Puritans relied on the Song of Songs along with New Testament passages such as the passion narratives to do a job on them, but they spent most of their time on heaven or hell. The soliloquy, a meditative style handed down from Augustine, entailed "a pleading the case with thyself."

Puritans complained of the straying heart just as contemplatives did in other ages. Baxter attributed such excursions to excuse-making, trifling, diversion to other concerns, and abruptly ending the work of meditation before it was well begun. His suggested remedy: "Use violence on your heart!"[36]

On the Way Together

What has been said up to now might leave the mistaken impression that Puritan, including Baptist, spirituality was almost wholly individual and private. Radicals, it is true, did go to an extreme there, just as extremists among monks did. For most Puritans, however, it is only partially true, for their spirituality also embraced a powerful sacramental and liturgical element that we cannot gloss over, and it spilled over into all of public life, from the family to the government of a commonwealth.

For one thing, the Sabbath played a powerful role in Puritan piety. Their commitment to it was motivated by much more than social necessity, changes in the character of labor, as Christopher Hill has argued.[37] Not even the interaction of Calvinism with social and economic forces would be adequate to explain the fervor with which Puritans fought to preserve it. They saw it, as Solberg has contended, as an integral part of their "program for revitalizing personal religion and building a holy commonwealth."[38] God commanded it as a part of the covenant. "The conscionable keeping of the Sabbath," Bishop Lewis Bayly judged, "is the Mother of all Religion, and good discipline in the Church. Take away the Sabbath . . . and what will shortly become of Religion. . . .?[39] Cotton Mather agreed:

> The Lord expresses the whole of *Religion*, under that Phrase, *keep my Sabbaths*.
> Tis true concerning both Persons and Peoples,
> That if *Religion* desirably flourish, *Sabbaths* will bee duely kept.

> But *Religion* will decay and wither, if Strictness
> about the *Sabbaths* do go.
>
> Indeed, not to keep *Sabbaths* exactly, is both
> the *Guise* of, and the *Way* to, the greatest Irreligion.
>
> As has been said of Prayer, *either Sin will make
> Men leave off praying, or Prayer will make Men leave off
> sinning:* so may wee say of the *Sabbath*.[40]

A devout Puritan such as John Winthrop, later governor of Massachusetts Bay Colony, could feel his "herte was very much unsettled" because he waited until after three o'clock Saturday afternoon (when devout Puritans began the Sabbath) to begin reading and prayer.[41]

Despite a high regard for preaching as *the* means for communication of grace, Puritans, like their mentor Calvin, also made much of the Lord's Supper. They took pains to prepare for reception, meditating on the worthiness of the sacrament, their personal worthiness for receiving it, and the means whereby one might become a worthy recipient. Puritan expectations of the sacrament were not far from those a Roman Catholic might have had. According to Lewis Bayly, one should look for forgiveness of sins, the Spirit and breath of grace, all saving graces, communion with Christ, a pledge of resurrection, assurance of everlasting life, and union with other Christians.[42] During the observance, he admonished, one should carry on "a sweet colloquy" with oneself. Even after returning home, one should reflect on whether he or she received diligently, was reconciled to God, and desired to receive again.

Puritans gained considerable notoriety for the discipline with which they sought to maintain the covenant. It is quite clear that they intended to create a visible society of saints that, without discipline, would have been quite impossible. Most would have subscribed to Milton's conviction on this matter.

> There is not that thing in the world of more grace and
> urgent importance throughout the whole life of [human-
> kind], than discipline. The flourishing and decaying of
> all civil societies, all the movements and turnings of
> human occasions are moved to and fro upon the axle
> of discipline. . . . Nor is there any sociable perfection
> in this life, civil or sacred, that can be above discipline;

> but she is that which with her musical chords preserves and holds all the parts thereof together. . . . Discipline is not only the removal of disorder, but if any visible shape can be given to divine things, the very visible shape and image of virtue.[43]

Such an outlook was rooted, as the last sentence suggests,[44] in Puritan concern for order. God has created an orderly world, down to the least item in creation. Humans, therefore, should regulate their society, else the latter might end up in chaos. Certainly the aim of a restored human community could be achieved only if Christians assumed their obligation to exercise discipline, and the brotherhood of preachers that stood at the core of Puritanism did not want to fail in this task.[45]

Puritan spirituality did not limit itself to the individual or even to the religious community. Heart religion had to manifest itself in transformed lifestyle and social concern. The work of grace in one's life is discovered, Faithful informed Talkative in *The Pilgrim's Progress*:

> (1) "by an experimental confession of his faith in Christ" and (2) "by a life answerable to that confession; to wit, a life of holiness, heart-holiness: family-holiness, (if he hath a family,) and by conversation-holiness in the world; which in the general teacheth him inwardly to abhor sin, and himself for that in secret; to suppress it in his family, and to promote holiness in the world: not by talk only, as an hypocrite or talkative person may do, but by a practical subjection in faith and love to the power of the word.[46]

Citing James 1:22, 27, Christian observed, "The soul of religion is the practical part: . . . At the Day of judgment one will not be asked, 'Did you believe?' but 'Were you *doers*, or *talkers* only?'"[47]

As part of a social revolution cresting during the seventeenth century, Puritans identified with the suffering and oppressed. In *The Plaine Man's Pathway to Heaven*, Arthur Dent listed "honest, just, and conscionable dealing in all our actions among men" among infallible signs of election. Sounding like a Latin American liberationist, he proceeded to catalogue areas in which oppression might occur:

- usury
- bribery
- racking of rents
- taking of excessive fines
- bargaining
- letting of leases
- letting of houses
- letting of grounds
- binding the poor to unreasonable covenants
- thrusting the poor out of their houses
- hiring the houses of the poor over their heads
- taking of fees.[48]

After heaping up a pile of scripture texts against such injustices, he enumerated the causes—cruelty, covetousness, hardheartedness, evil conscience, and the Devil—and cures—pity, contentment, tender affections, a good conscience, and much prayer.[49]

Being a part of the "industrious sort" gave a peculiar twist to the Puritan view of wealth. They did not regard wealth as a blessing and poverty as a curse, as often accused. From Calvin, rather, they inherited a concept of calling that encouraged ceaseless effort. One's calling belonged to the divine order of things. Its primary goal was to serve God and humankind, not to amass wealth. Thus one had to pursue a vocation with diligence, zeal, and persistence to the glory of God and out of gratitude to God. Should one prosper, one must be a good steward. A good steward would live frugally—the Puritan version of monastic asceticism. Good stewardship would not mean careless liberality to the poor. Puritans were severe toward vagabonds and freeloaders, and Cotton Mather was more the exception than the rule in his preoccupation with the poor in his parish.[50]

Puritan/Baptist Spirituality
in Retrospect and Prospect

Puritanism has often been caricatured from its negative side: "Don't dance. Don't drink. Don't smoke. Don't Chew. Don't go with those who do." Admittedly some of the caricature fits when one evaluates Puritanism in terms of convention rather than in terms of tradition. The Puritan tradition, by which I mean its essence, was commendable and laudable, entailing a spirited search for heart religion manifested in transformation of both individuals and society. Like the prophets of old, the Puritans wanted holiness and justice to "roll down like waters." Like Jesus, they too denounced play acting at religion by legalistic and trivialistic observances that diverted people from sincere and authentic commitment; saying, "Lord! Lord!" mattered little if you did not do what he said.

Where did Puritanism fail? Not in its intention surely. If so, you would have to fault biblical spirituality, which Puritans sought so assiduously to emulate and to realize in their own lives—or medieval spirituality that they borrowed from in so many ways. No, if they fell short of their aims, it would have been because they were so ambitious as to be unrealistic. They wanted and they expected by grace to be a society of redeemed and saintly humans, restoring the order disrupted by the Fall; being faithful to the covenant. This is why discipline was so crucial. In their zeal, however, they forgot some of their most basic tenets.

The Puritans—Baptists included—were voluntarists. They believed that the sovereign God alone has a claim on the conscience.[51] Only if people freely enter into covenant, therefore, with God and with one another, can discipline be exercised. What happens when they no longer "own the covenant"? This is the crucial question the Puritans confronted within a generation, and they had to admit failure of their noble experiment with the "half-way covenant."

Those who had remonstrated with the Church of England for being only "halfly reformed" were no more than that themselves. If they had remembered their premise about human nature, far more realistic than their goal for society, they might have seen greater wisdom in the monastic vision. The monks did not try to reform everyone, a whole society. They, being voluntarists too, were content to work with those who were willing to withdraw from society into disciplined communities.

Or the Puritans might also have settled for the Anabaptist model of the "gathered church" composed only of the regenerate, as Baptists did. By expanding their vision to the outer margins of society, they became coercive. Magistrates imposed covenant obligations, religious as well as civil, on all and sundry. They levied fines, imprisoned, whipped, and even hanged persons who stepped outside the lines. By 1700 the Puritan vision, so luminous at one time, was scarcely a flicker.

What can we learn from the Puritan experience that might help Baptists deal with the crisis in their spirituality today?

26

Some well-meaning Christians, including Baptists, seem to suggest that we might return to the Puritan era and again recapture the vision and program for the United States. Godliness and holiness should again pervade the White House, the Capitol, schools, businesses, homes, along with churches. The American will stand as the bulwark of a Christian commonwealth against the tide of godless communism and secularism. Appealing as those words may sound to some ears, they ignore the failure of the Puritan plan.

The Puritans' own realism—"We have no enduring city here"— should have tempered their effort to realize the Kingdom of God in Old or New England, at least putting some control on misguided zeal to mold all and sundry in one mold. Unfortunately it took the deterioration of religion to remind them again of the validity of their voluntarist principle: To be authentic, faith must be free. Early Baptists grasped that point the best.

If we can keep this principle in the forefront, then the Puritan/Baptist spirituality we began with can help us. By way of the Puritan tradition we can find our way back to the Catholic mainstream, for that is where Puritanism headed in its drive to obtain a fuller reformation. The essence of Puritan spirituality is also the essence of Christian spirituality rooted in the Scriptures. Indeed a student of the history of Christian spirituality will find little that is new in Puritan spirituality. For the Puritans the newness lay in rediscovery, in the joy of coming once more upon a discarded item long forgotten, and in the zeal with which they pursued the old. Many persons are having a similar experience today in this era of the "New Pentecost" introduced by Pope John XXIII.

Notes

[1] E. Glenn Hinson, "Puritan Spirituality," in *Protestant Spiritual Traditions*, ed. Frank C. Senn (Mahwah, NJ: Paulist Press, 1986), 165-182.

[2] Lewis Bayly, *The Practise of Pietie*, 3rd ed. (London: J. Hodges, 1613), 163.

[3] John Bunyan, *The Pilgrim's Progress*, ch. 20. On Puritan fascination with Hebrews, see William Perkins' *A Cloud of Faithful Witnesses, a Commentary on Hebrews xi* (London: H. Lownes, 1608).

[4] See David E. Stannard, *The Puritan Way of Death: A Study in Religion, Culture, and Social Change* (New York: Oxford University Press, 1977), 72-95.

[5] Christopher Hill, *Society and Puritanism in Pre-Revolutionary England*, 2nd ed. (New York: Schocken Books, 1964, 1967), 20, 129, 132.

[6] Cotton Mather, *Diary of Cotton Mather* (New York: Frederick Ungar Publishing Co, n.d.), I: 262f.

[7] 35 Eliz. Cap. I; cited by Hill, *Society and Puritanism*, 447.

[8] Hill, *Society and Puritanism*, 449.

[9] J. Mayne, *The English Catechism Explained*, 3rd ed. (1623), 278.

[10] Richard Baxter, *The Saints' Everlasting Rest* in Doubleday Devotional Classics, ed. E. Glenn Hinson (Garden City, NJ: Doubleday & Co, Inc, 1978), I: 90.

[11] Mather, *Diary*, I: 87f.

[12] See Baxter, *The Saints' Everlasting Rest*, I: 55-70.

[13] Ibid., 86.

[14] See my fuller reconstruction in *Doubleday Devotional Classics*, I: 211-212.

[15] In *The Creeds and Platforms of Congregationalism*, ed. Williston Walker (Boston: Pilgrim Press, 1960), 116.

[16] Bayly, *The Practise of Pietie*, 234-290.

[17] Baxter, *The Saints' Everlasting Rest*, 112.

[18] John Bunyan, *The Pilgrim's Progress*, in *Doubleday Devotional Classics*, I: 355.

[19] Bayly, *The Practise of Pietie*, 156-157. According to *Paterna: The Autobiography of Cotton Mather*, ed. Ronald A. Bosco (Delmar, NY: Scholars' Facsimiles and Reprints, 1976), 6, Mather read fifteen chapters a day as a child of age seven or eight!

[20] Mather, *Diary*, I: 103, II: 578.

[21] On the literature of Puritan spirituality, see Owen C. Watkins, *The Puritan Experience* (London: Routledge & Kegan Paul, 1972).

[22] John Bunyan, *I Will Pray with the Spirit*, ed. Richard L. Greaves (Oxford: Clarendon Press, 1976), 235.

[23] Mather, *Diary* I: 110; Mather, *Paterna*, 16.

[24] *Diary* I: 187, 233, 227

[25] Ibid., 199.

[26] Ibid., 187.

[27] *Massachusetts Archives* XI.8; cited in Mather, *Diary*, I: 22, n. 2.

[28] Mather, *Diary*, I: 237.

[29] Baxter, *The Saints' Everlasting Rest*, 120-29.

[30] For a more detailed comparison of Puritan and earlier disciplines, see Charles Hambrick-Stowe, *The Practice of Piety: Puritan Devotional Disciplines in Seventeenth-Century New England* (Chapel Hill: University of North Carolina Press, 1982), 25-39.

[31] Baxter, *The Saints' Everlasting Rest*, 130-138.

[32] Meister Eckhart, *Counsels of Discernment*, 2, in *Meister Eckhart*, trans. Edmund College, OSA, and Bernard McGinn, Classics of Western Spirituality (New York: Paulist Press, 1981), 248.

[33] Baxter, *The Saints' Everlasting Rest*, 143.

[34] Ibid., 159.

[35] I have explored the connection between Ignatian and Puritan approaches in "Ignatian and Puritan Prayer: Surprising Similarities; A Comparison of Ignatius Loyola and Richard Baxter on Meditation," *The Merton Annual*, 20: 79-92.

[36] Baxter, *The Saints' Everlasting Rest*, 169-173.

[37] Hill, *Society and Puritanism*,145-218.

[38] Winton U. Solberg, *Redeeming the Time* (Cambridge, MA: Harvard University Press, 1977), 31.

[39] Bayly, *The Practise of Piety*, 513.

[40] Mather, *Diary* I: 30.

[41] *Winthrop Papers*, 162; cited by Solberg, *Redeeming the Time*, 69.

[42] Bayly, *The Practise of Piety*, 664-791. On Calvin's high view of eucharist, see Kilian McDonnell, OSB, *John Calvin, the Church, and the Eucharist* (Princeton, NJ: Princeton University Press, 1967), 223ff.

[43] John Milton, *Prose Works* (Bohn Edition), II: 442-442; cited by Hill, *Society and Puritanism*, 275.

[44] Cf. Stephen Foster, *Their Solitary Way* (New Haven and London: Yale University Press, 1971), 11-40.

[45] Patrick Collison, *The Elizabethan Puritan Movement* (London and New York: Methuen, 1967), 59, has traced the origins of the Puritan party in England to preachers who regarded the Church of England as only "halfly reformed." Composed mostly of persons who had spent some time of exile either in Zürich or Geneva, this fellowship complained about the Elizabethan Settlement as regards the role of preaching, the importance of Bible study, discipline, and ecclesiastical preferments. By 1566, under royal pressure toward uniformity, they began to emerge as an underground movement. These "privy" congregations attached to their preachers rather than to parish churches emphasized disciplined observance of the covenant.

[46] John Bunyan, *The Pilgrim's Progress*, 387.

[47] Ibid., 384.

[48] Pages 182-183 of 2012 reprint.

[49] Ibid., 197.

[50] See Foster, *Their Solitary Way*, 148-152.

[51] Baptists' *Second London Confession* (1677), which virtually duplicated *The Westminster Confession* (1646), declared: "God alone is Lord of the Conscience, and hath left it free from the Doctrines and Commandments of men which are in any way contrary to the Word, or not contained in it. So that to Believe such Doctrines, or obey such Commands out of Conscience, is to betray true liberty of Conscience; and the requiring of an implicit Faith, and absolute and blind Obedience, is to destroy Liberty of Conscience, and Reason also" (XXI.2; in *Baptist Confessions of Faith*, ed. William L. Lumpkin [Philadelphia: Judson Press, 1959], 279-280).

Part 3

Conversionist Spirituality
Overloading the Front End of the Spiritual Life

I n part two I spoke about Puritan/Baptist spirituality as essentially a continuation of the contemplative tradition of Christianity prior to the Reformation of the sixteenth century. The contemplative tradition emphasized attentiveness to God, the approach to spirituality most threatened by the distractedness so characteristic of the modern day. In trying to make our major point of the critical importance of recovering our attentiveness to God, it will be helpful to look more closely at the developments in Christian spirituality that pushed the contemplative tradition aside and replaced it with a spirituality that focused on getting God to do what we want rather than our doing what God wants.

I see two big steps in this direction. The first one originated during the Great Awakening, gained momentum during the Second Great Awakening or frontier revivals, and reached its peak in the period Kenneth Scott Latourette called "the great century" of missions. In this phase Baptist spirituality shifted focus from the total process of being reformed and transformed in the image of God to the front end of the process, or conversion. Simultaneously, the measure of the Christian life changed from demonstration in the way we lived to demonstration in how fervently we witnessed to others.

The second step, which had an especially heavy impact on Baptists in America, where 80 percent of Baptists reside, is connected with the fact that Baptists grew up alongside American business enterprise, starting with the railroads in the mid-nineteenth century and proceeding unchecked until our own day. This step, which I will deal with in the next section, begot a pragmatic approach to the covenant we enter into with God. We negotiate rather than place ourselves at God's disposal.

In this third section I will try to explicate how we developed our obsession with "conversion" and "witness" to the detriment of a more well-rounded, full-bodied attentiveness to God that should characterize people of the covenant.

The Great Awakening

Much of the contemplative spirituality continued in conversionist spirituality, but the Great Awakening of the eighteenth century and the Second Great Awakening of the early nineteenth century effected some significant changes in the spirituality of many Baptists. Some of the shift was healthy. Experience of "conversion" by vast numbers raised serious questions about Calvin's doctrine of "election" that attributed to an "eternal decree" that some would be "saved" but others would be "damned." The evidence seemed to say that *all* had a chance, and this pumped new energy into their spiritual search.

The central conundrum that stirred the waters of the Awakening was whether "religious affections," that is, experiences, could be trusted, especially because they sometimes took bizarre forms such as swooning, speaking in tongues, and barking up trees. Many disputed the "excesses." Jonathan Edwards, pastor of the Congregational Church in Northampton, Massachusetts, where the Awakening reached its peak about 1740-1742,[1] stepped up to defend them, though with some caution. In *A Treatise Concerning Religious Affections*, he underlined that authentic religious experience originates with God. To him this meant there might be false or misleading signs of religious affections, that is, those that lack "true grace." He listed a dozen that he thought gave neither positive nor negative evidence and therefore should be discounted[2] and a dozen more by which to distinguish true from false affections.[3]

Judging by the amount of space Edwards allotted the latter, two held a preeminent place in his mind. Truly "gracious affections," he said, "arise from those influences and operations on the heart that are spiritual, supernatural, and divine"[4] and they "have their exercise and fruit in Christian practice."[5] Ultimately, he concluded in agreement with John

Bunyan, practice of piety matters most. "False discoveries and affections don't go deep enough to reach and govern the springs of [human] actions and practice."[6] True ones do precisely that.

Edwards rested his case for the experiential aspects of the Great Awakening on *The Diary of David Brainerd,* which he edited. Afflicted with tuberculosis, Brainerd (1718-1747) spent his last days in Edwards' home cared for by Edwards' daughter, Jerusha, who died at age eighteen, less than a year after Brainerd himself. In the Brainerd story one can see in embryo the two major shifts from the contemplative to the conversionist spirituality—signs of conversion and missionary zeal as *sine qua non.*

As Brainerd himself evaluated his religious pilgrimage, he experienced two "conversions." The first, stretched out over a number of years, was more or less perfunctory; the second profound, agonizing, and genuine.

The first began with his "conviction of sin" at age seven or eight, perhaps at the time of his father's death. For a time he applied himself zealously to "performance of religious duties" but soon lapsed. At age thirteen he was "roused out of this carnal security" by the death of his mother. He had to assume responsibility for the care of his siblings. On his nineteenth birthday he dedicated himself anew to prayer and other religious duties. What Brainerd regarded as his real "conversion" grew out of the Awakening going on around him in 1738 and 1739. The profound experience he had longed and struggled for so intensely came at last on July 12, 1739. It resembled Isaiah's call (Isa. 6:1-10), Paul's ecstatic experience (2 Cor. 12:1-10, Acts 9:3-9), and the experience of mystics through the ages. It merits quotation at length:

> [A]s I was walking in a dark thick grove, unspeakable glory seemed to open to the view and apprehension of my soul. . . . My soul rejoiced with joy unspeakable, to see such a God, such a glorious divine Being; and I was inwardly pleased and satisfied that he should be God over all for ever and ever. My soul was captivated and delighted with the excellency, loveliness, greatness, and other perfections of God, that I was even swallowed up in him; at least to the degree, that I had not thought (as I remember) at first, about my own salvation, and scarce reflected that there was such a creature as myself.

Thus God, I trust, brought me to a hearty disposition to exalt him, and set him on the throne, and principally and ultimately to aim at his honour and glory, as King of the universe. I continued in this state of inward joy, peace, and astonishment, till near dark, without any sensible abatement; and then began to think and examine what I had seen; and felt sweetly composed in my mind all the evening following. I felt myself in a new world, and everything about me appeared with a different aspect from what it was wont to do.[7]

As William James analyzed this, a more powerful opposite affection overpowered Brainerd's fear, guilt, anger, despair, and other undesirable affections.[8]

In September, Brainerd entered Yale, fearful of further lapses. A number of divine "visits" counterbalanced his ambition in his studies. Sadly, in August 1740 he began to experience symptoms of the tuberculosis that eventually claimed his life. Returning for his second year at Yale, he "felt the power of religion almost daily, for the space of six weeks,"[9] but, in late January 1741, "grew more cold and dull" as a result of his studiousness.[10] As the end of February, however, "a great and general Awakening spread itself over the college." Along with others, Brainerd got carried away in his enthusiasm and committed the deed that led to his expulsion and loaded him with an almost unbearable sense of guilt and remorse. The incident, criticism of a professor as having "no more grace (piety) than this chair," became a watershed for the brief remainder of his life.

Although he wrote a letter of apology to the rector and trustees and the governors of the college readmitted him with restrictions, the expulsion plunged him into depression. Whatever relief he experienced resulted from his appointment to the Indian mission by the Society for Promoting Christian Knowledge of the Church of England. He eventually had phenomenal success, but he paid a high price getting there, as recounted in this entry to his *Diary*.

My circumstances are such that I have no comfort of
any kind, but what I have in God. I live in the most
lonesome wilderness; have but one single person to
converse with that can speak English. Most of the talk
I hear is either Highland Scotch, or Indian. I have no
fellow-christians to whom I may unbosom myself, or
lay open my spiritual sorrows; with whom I may take
sweet counsel in conversation about heavenly things,
and join in social prayer. I live poorly with regard to the
comforts of life: most of my diet consists of boiled corn,
hasty-pudding, &c. I lodge on a bundle of straw, my
labour is hard and extremely difficult, and I have little
appearance of success, to comfort me. The Indians have
no land to live on, but what the Dutch people lay claim
to; and these threaten to drive them off. They have no
regard to the souls of the poor Indians; and by what I
can learn, they hate me because I come to preach to
them. But that which makes all my difficulties grievous
to be borne, is, that God hides his face from me.[11]

To be among the Indians, he exulted on October 5, 1745, is "like being
admitted into [God's] family, and to the enjoyment of [God's] divine
presence."[12] His health broke down completely in 1747, and he died
October 9.

Debate over the legitimacy of experiential aspects of the Awakening
sundered religious bodies. Even Jonathan Edwards' carefully reasoned case
for "religious affections" failed to prevent the rending of Congregationalists,
Presbyterians, and Baptists. The strictest Calvinists among Baptists,
called "Regular," refused to make room for experiential spirituality. The
"Separate" or "New Light" Baptists, who accepted the shift, comprised the
larger stream of those who migrated to the South.[13] Those who looked to
British Calvinist John Gill (1697-1771) for guidance held fast to the earlier
Puritan model with little wavering. Gill himself, however, represented a
transitional figure who respected Edwards' views.

In a recent study of Gill's spirituality, Gregory A. Wills has contended
that Gill, like earlier Puritans, considered heart religion "the essence of
Christianity."[14] He countered the moralism and rationalism of his day
by insisting on "the fire that burned in love to Christ."[15] Like medieval

contemplatives, he sustained his contention in a series of sermons on the Song of Songs, which he published in 1728. He conceived Christian spirituality as "a love song between Christ and those he redeemed."[16] He placed the ravishing love of God and the beauty of Christ at the center of his spirituality. The chief goal of spirituality is love to Christ and delight in his beauty. The way to the goal is through daily communion with Christ. That communion leads to worship. To attain the goal of loving God requires knowledge, and, not surprisingly to those who know Gill, knowledge of doctrine. Doctrine, as he understood it, however, is "spiritual and experimental knowledge of God . . . which leads men [and women] to mind and savour spiritual things."[17] Finally, spirituality needs the institutional church, the locus of divine power, and the church's observances, especially the Lord's Supper.

Although Wills saw a striking resemblance to Edwards' emphasis on "religious affections" in Gill's spirituality, we must recognize that Gill's *Exposition of the Book of Solomon's Song* antedated Edwards' treatise by eighteen years and thus would not have been indebted to it. The fact is, Wills admits, "Gill felt ambivalence toward the universal appeal of the gospel."[18] Preachers should proclaim the doctrines of the gospel, but they should not offer grace or forgiveness. That is the very point that the Awakening put to a severe test.

Loosening Calvinist Fetters on Missions

Jonathan Edwards' influence weighed much more heavily on Andrew Fuller (1754-1815) and, through him, on other Baptists. Although reared in a family of "dissenters of the Calvinistic persuasion," Fuller did not affiliate with Baptists until April 1770, a month after witnessing the administration of baptism by immersion for the first time.

In the midst of a theological controversy that split the Soham church where he was baptized, he gained the confidence of the congregation and was called as pastor. The controversy revolved in part around the question as to whether the gospel is to be preached to all or only to the "elect," for Robert Hall Sr., who delivered his ordination charge, encouraged him to read Edwards' writings.

In 1776 Fuller came into contact with John Sutcliff of Olney and John Ryland of Northampton, "who, Fuller recorded, partly by reflection, and partly by reading the writings of Edwards, Bellamy, Brainerd, etc., had begun to doubt the system of false Calvinism to which they had been inclined when they first entered on the ministry, or rather to be decided against it."[19] Separated from them by sixty or seventy miles, however, Fuller worked out independently the substance of his epochal treatise titled *The Gospel Worthy of All Acceptation*," published in 1784. Fuller's balancing of divine grace and human responsibility signaled a way to remove the burden that lay heavy on the heart of William Carey, namely, whether it was appropriate to use means for conversion of the unconverted. Carey's 1792 *Inquiry into the Use of Means for the Conversion of the Heathen* gave a resounding yes.

The New Accents in Baptist Spirituality

Conversionist spirituality, therefore, injected a couple of new accents into Baptist spirituality that help one to understand better what has created a mania for missions in much of Baptist life but especially among Baptists in the South. One of these is a shift from the goal of Christian life and the way to the goal to an almost exclusive concern for the gateway to the way, that is, conversion. Confirmation of this development is clear in the fact that the invitation has replaced baptism as the dominant sacrament ("means of grace") in Baptist churches in the South.[20]

As in frontier revivals, the object is to get people to respond to the exhortation. Not much attention is given in many churches to the personal account of religious experience; it suffices to come forward and declare oneself. When linked with the assurance "Once saved, always saved," nothing more need be done. Take the bus and leave the driving up to Jesus!

Closely associated with this focus on "conversion," certification of conversion also underwent a change. Whereas in contemplative spirituality living what one believed verified authenticity and the truly devout were the exemplars of piety, in conversionist spirituality witness to others became the ultimate test and preachers or missionaries the model Christians. One can see this transition manifesting itself in the biographical memoirs of Baptists already in the period of the Great Awakening (about 1720-1760) and frontier revivals (about 1790-1820). John Gano's autobiography offers a sterling example.

The John Gano Story

Gano, whose life spanned both "awakenings" (1722-1804), majored on two things: his conversion and his calling to serve as an itinerant preacher or missionary of the Baptist denomination. The conversion story sounds much like David Brainerd's.

The son of a devout Presbyterian father and Baptist mother, Gano spoke of "some severe convictions of sins" early in his life.[21] These did not last, however, and he lapsed into "youthful vanity and sin" about which his mother confronted him and he reformed, but only momentarily.[22] When he was fifteen, the death of his twenty-year-old brother Stephen after a brief illness "greatly engaged my resolution to seek an acquaintance, if possible, with Christ."[23] His resolve lapsed again. Two or three years later, dysentary claimed the lives of another brother and two sisters, one of whom was also twenty. A prediction that three of his father's children would die at age twenty haunted him thereafter. Nevertheless, for a time, he continued "more vile and vain than ever" whenever he could dispel such gloomy thoughts.[24]

At Christmas just before Gano reached age nineteen, foregoing an evening of fun with buddies, he went to church and heard a sermon that set him to thinking how improper it was to live in open rebellion "if a day was regarded as the birth of Christ, a holy Savior, through whom alone we could look for salvation."[25] Before the year was over, he "was brought under serious impressions" in conversation with someone he respected for his faith. He endeavored earnestly to obtain pardon for his sins and "embraced every opportunity in my power, in attending preaching, reading godly books, and praying either mentally or aloud."[26]

What Gano learned was, however, that he needed a change of heart that only God's grace could effect. He remained in a state of grief regarding his alienation of heart for some time until he was overwhelmed by the realization that Christ's life, death, and mediation assured the way of salvation despite his ingratitude. Although he wavered for a time still, a sermon on the text, "Jesus, thou Son of David, have mercy on me," gripped him and "opened the way of salvation, the suitableness, fullness, and willingness of God."[27] He dated his conversion from that experience.

From that point on, Gano hastened to give the validation of his conversion experience in witness. Where earlier Baptist spiritual biographies such as Bunyan's *Grace Abounding* focused on personal struggle and growth, Gano's reported almost exclusively on his effort to evangelize others. Even before he joined a church, he set about to warn other young people of the wrath of God and to direct them to Christ and "the method of salvation through Him."[28]

When it came time to settle on a church home, he sought the counsel of the eminent Presbyterian leader Gilbert Tennent (1703-1764), the oldest son of William, founder of the "Log College" (Princeton), but he could not find support for infant baptism in scriptures and decided to join the Baptist church. Isaac Eaton, newly called as pastor of the famous Hopewell Church, instructed him in classics and guided his preparation for ministry.[29]

Where scriptures had come to the aid of Bunyan in fighting his battle with depression and guiding him toward the heavenly city, they now came to Gano's aid to send him forth to preach. He bought a plantation and started farming. Spending much time in prayer and meditation on scriptures, the words "Go forth and preach the Gospel" (cf. Mark 16:15) "powerfully impressed my mind."[30]

When doubts assailed him, he got many scriptural reinforcements:

- "It is I, be not afraid—be not faithless, but believing."
  (Matt. 14:27; Mark 6:50)
- "Thou shalt speak to many people." (cf. Rev. 10:11)
- "I will send thee far hence." (Acts 22:21)
- "Say not I am a child, I will be with thee. I will be with thy lips. And thou shalt speak to all, to whom I send thee." (cf. Jer. 7:27)
- "I have made thee this day, a brazen wall and an iron sinew." (cf. Jer. 1:18)[31]

When he continued to resist or ignore the call and go about his farming, texts from the Bible "weighed heavily" on his mind:

- "Warn the people, or their blood will I require at your hands." (cf. Ezek 33:3)
- "If I do this willingly, I have my reward, but if not a dispensation of the gospel is committed unto me." (1 Cor. 9:17)
- "Necessity is laid upon me, woe is me if I preach not the gospel." (1 Cor. 9:16)[32]

Though he was plagued still by doubts, his pastor, Isaac Eaton, informed the Hopewell Church of Gano's growing sense of calling to preach the gospel. He proceeded then in the next several years to pursue the studies this task required. Illness prevented his capping off his preparation at Princeton College. Doctors and friends advised him instead to relax his studying. So he proceeded to journey southwards to preach at Opekon Creek Church in Virginia. He returned to New Jersey, where he was licensed and ordained.

The remainder of his memoirs recounted Gano's remarkable ministry, which entailed much travel from the beginning. What held his attention in telling the story was the concern at the heart of the Great Awakening and frontier revival, that is, conversions and additions to the church. Regarding his stay at the Jersey Settlement in Yadkin, North Carolina, for instance, he recorded:

> They had finished a meeting-house, and had began a parsonage-house; and they seemed disposed to do anything to render me happy. Their church, which at first consisted of only twenty-six members, were speedily increased; and a hopeful work began. At every church-meeting there was a number who offered themselves. My usual services on Lord's days were preaching three times; and I gave a lecture weekly. The church being too small to accommodate the people who attended, an addition was made to it. The church, at this time, had increased to two hundred in number.[33]

Gano kept his attention largely on military matters in recounting his years as a chaplain to colonial forces during the American Revolution (1776-1783) except to slip in occasional reports on sermons. When he did, he often hinted at his disappointment at soldiers' piety. On July 4, 1779 he related that "the soldiery behaved with the most decency that I ever knew them to during the war." He then added, "Some of them usually absented themselves from worship on Lord's day, and the only punishment they were subjected to was the digging up of stumps, which, in some instance, had a good effect."[34]

Returning after the war to New York City to gather a badly depleted flock, he reported, "The Lord looked graciously upon us: we soon had a large congregation, numbers were sensibly convicted, and many were brought to bow the knee to King Jesus."[35] The pitiful economic circumstances the war left him in, however, made the frontier attractive, and in 1787 Gano yielded to pleas of William Wood, pastor of Limestone Church in Mason County, Kentucky, to help there. Later he moved his family to Lexington to serve as pastor of Town Fork Church and then, while still pastor there, to Frankfort.

Inasmuch as the last part of his ministry took place during the early days of the Second Great Awakening, which reached its peak near Lexington around 1800-1806, it is not surprising to see the conversionist/call to preach heightened in descriptions of Gano's spiritual life.

After a stroke paralyzed him in September 1798, Gano discontinued his memoirs. In completing them, his son Stephen kept the same conversionist perspective. He noted that although his father remained paralyzed, he "preached several times supported in his bed; and attended every Association, except one, until his death."[36] He cited a William Hickman, who added that when traveling preachers called, talked, and preached, Gano "would sit in his chair and exhort to duty, and to flee from vice."[37]

A year after his stroke, Gano was taken to Town Fork and Bryants Station to preach. When he grew too tired while preaching, "some friend would support him" and "he would preach with renewed ardor."[38] In the midst of the frontier revival, "When a little recovered, he would venture to the meeting house, on horseback, where he would exhort, preach, pray and give counsel, sound and good, while he was supported by two persons to steady him. At other times he would go to the water side at the administration of baptism, and advocate that mode."[39] To the very end, his son remarked of his last day, August 10, 1804, "He appeared permanently fixed on Jesus as the Rock of Ages."[40]

The Consequences of the Change

Throughout my life in the Baptist community I have heard paeans of praise for the changes in outlook wrought by the awakenings. Mission professors at Southern Seminary could scarcely find words adequate to laud Andrew Fuller and William Carey for breaking the stranglehold on Baptist mission work implicit in Calvinism, notably the Calvinism of John Gill's *The Body of Divinity*. Two dormitories at Southern Seminary feted the pioneers in American Baptist mission work, Adoniram Judson and Luther Rice. The Southern Baptist Convention, more than any other group a product of the Separate Baptists of the Great Awakening and of the frontier revivals, elevated Lottie Moon and Annie Armstrong to permanent sainthood by collecting annual offerings for missions under their names.

Please understand: I do not want my critique of the conversionist model in spirituality to be interpreted as a broadside against missions, the mania of many Baptists. You will recognize, too, that I am not an enthusiast for the neo-Calvinism now rearing its head among Baptists in the South. Calvin was not their kind of Calvinist. Their Calvinism goes back to the hyper-Calvinist Synod of Dort, and I think it does threaten the mission endeavors of Baptists, particularly by the revival of its determinism: "God has predetermined everything. Why do we need to do anything?"

No, the only thing I want to raise question about here is whether the two significant shifts in spirituality from the contemplative model has caused us to reverse the order of things and thus helped to push God out toward the periphery of our spiritual lives. That, you see, is where I locate our crisis, in God the forgotten one.

Actually, in our obsession with evangelism and missions, we haven't forgotten God altogether; we've just wanted God to do what *we* want God to do. Prayer, the central thing in spirituality, is not listening to God and asking God what God wants so much as it is informing God about what we intend to do and demanding that God get behind us in it. Meanwhile, our obsession with getting people to make "decisions" has lessened our concern with what happens thereafter, with whether the love of God will continue to grow in understanding and in every sensitivity so that we may have a sense of things that really matter and attain purity of heart and produce fruits of righteousness that rebound to the glory and praise of God. You will recognize that as my paraphrase of Paul's prayer for the Philippians (1:9-11). It should still apply to us today.

Notes

[1] See Edwin Scott Gaustad, *The Great Awakening in New England* (New York: Harper & Brothers, 1957), 42-60.

[2] Listed briefly, these were: (1) fervency of affections, (2) bodily effects, (3) fervency in talking about religion, (4) that they weren't self-induced, (5) that they come with texts of scripture darting into the mind, (6) that there is an appearance of love in them, (7) that there are a lot of them, (8) that comforts and joys follow awakenings and convictions of conscience

in a certain order, (9) that they dispose people to spend a lot of time in religion or external duties of worship, (10) that they dispose people to praise and glorify God a lot, (11) that they make people confident of a good relationship with God, and (12) that the manifestations may impress the truly devout.

[3] The distinguishing signs of truly gracious and holy affections were: (1) They are "spiritual, supernatural, and divine." (2) They aim at divine realities and not promotion of self or self-interest. (3) They are "truly holy" and "primarily founded on the loveliness of the moral excellency of divine things." (4) They arise from divine enlightenment of the mind. (5) They are attended "with a reasonable and spiritual conviction of the reality and certainty of divine things." (6) They are attended by "evangelical humiliation." (7) They are attended by a change of nature. (8) They tend to and are attended by "the lamb-like, dove-like spirit and temper of Jesus Christ." (9) They "soften the heart and are attended and followed with a Christian tenderness of spirit." (10) They exhibit "beautiful symmetry and proportion." (11) The higher they are raised, "the more is a spiritual appetite and longing of the soul after spiritual attainments increased." (12) They "have their exercise and fruit in Christian practice."

[4] Jonathan Edwards, *A Treatise Concerning Religious Affections*, ed. John E. Smith (Boston: S. Kneeland and T. Green, 1746; New Haven, CT: Yale University Press, 1959), 265.

[5] Ibid., 383.

[6] Ibid.

[7] *The Diary of David Brainerd* in Doubleday Devotional Classics, ed. E. Glenn Hinson (Garden City, NJ: Doubleday & Co, Inc, 1978), II: 380-381.

[8] William James, *Varieties of Religious Experience* (New York: Collier Books, 1961), 177-178, 206.

[9] *Diary*, Hinson, II: 384.

[10] *Diary;* Hinson, II: 385.

[11] *Diary*, May 18, 1743; Hinson, II: 412-413.

[12] *Diary*, Oct. 5, 1745; Hinson, II: 493-494.

[13] See William L. Lumpkin, *Baptist Foundations in the South: Tracing through the Separates the Influence of the Great Awakening 1754-1787* (Nashville: Broadman Press, 1961).

[14] Gregory A. Wills, "A Fire that Burns Within: The Spirituality of John Gill," in *John Gill: The Life and Thought of John Gill (1697-1771): A Tercentennial Appreciation*, ed. Michael A. G. Haykin (Leiden and New York: E. G. Brill, 1997), 192.

[15] Ibid.

[16] Ibid., 193.

[17] John Gill, *Body of Doctrinal and Practical Divinity*, 709.

[18] Wills, "A Fire," 208.

[19] In Arthur Kirkby, *Andrew Fuller (1754-1815)*, (London: Independent Press Ltd, 1961), 7.

[20] See Bill J. Leonard, "Getting Saved in America: Conversion Event in a Pluralistic Culture," *Review & Expositor* 82 (1985), 123-125.

[21] John Gano, *Biographical Memoirs of the Late Rev. John Gano*, ed. Stephen Gano in *The Life and Ministry of John Gano, 1727-1804*, ed. Terry Wolever (Springfield, MO: Particular Baptist Press, 1998), 19.

[22] Ibid., 20.

[23] Ibid., 21.

[24] Ibid., 22.

[25] Ibid.

[26] Ibid., 23.

[27] Ibid., 25.

[28] Ibid.
[29] Ibid., 31.
[30] Ibid., 33.
[31] Ibid., 33-34.
[32] Ibid., 35.
[33] Ibid., 74-75.
[34] Ibid., 86.
[35] Ibid., 96f.
[36] Ibid., 107.
[37] Ibid., 109.
[38] Ibid.
[39] Ibid., 109f.
[40] Ibid., 111.

Part 4

Corporate Spirituality
Baptist Spirituality Going off the Rails

Baptists have been particularly vulnerable to the effects of culture in the American setting where more than 80 percent of all Baptists live. Nowhere does this trait manifest itself more clearly than in the evolution of Baptist spirituality in the Southern Baptist Convention. This body, formed in 1845, grew up with American enterprise and steeped itself in the pragmatism that the business model injected into American social consciousness.

Business Baptists

Culture, to be sure, puts its mark on all religious groups. Churches shaped long ago in other cultures—Roman Catholic, Orthodox, Anglican—however, prove much less susceptible to its impact today than those that favor congregational polity and, as it were, grow up in a young and developing environment such as the American colonies and the United States of America. The hierarchical structure of the Roman Catholic Church, molded chiefly during the first several centuries of its existence in the Roman Empire, serves as a counterweight against contemporary culture. The congregational polity of Baptist churches has not provided a similar counterweight; instead, it has adapted itself to shifts in culture.

During their early days in England and in the American colonies, for instance, Baptists formed associations for purposes of fellowship, mutual support, education, doctrine, and so on. In the eighteenth century, societies formed to support single concerns. As mania for missions grew in the late eighteenth century, Baptists formed societies aimed chiefly at support of their evangelistic enterprise, at first abroad and then at home. That is how the so-called Triennial Convention of Baptists came into being in 1814 as a result of the work of Adoniram and Ann Haseltine Judson in Burma and the frenetic fundraising of Luther Rice in the homeland. A Home Society formed in 1832.

Business burgeoned in America in the nineteenth century. When the Southern Baptist Convention was born in 1845, it did not follow the earlier society method of organization to achieve one purpose. Instead, it adopted the multi-purpose convention model used already in South Carolina. At its beginning the Southern Baptist Convention created two boards—a Foreign Mission Board and a Domestic Mission Board—to carry on its work. In 1891, after several abortive attempts at developing a publishing enterprise, it added the Sunday School Board. Where did such designations as convention and board come from?

"Convention" doubtless entered ecclesiastical usage from the political arena. It especially designates large gatherings. "Board," however, came out of corporate usage. Boards managed railroads, steel companies, cotton mills, banks, and all those other businesses that gradually spread across the United States, including the South, once the economy cranked up again after the Civil War.

Industry boomed in the North, but, until well into the twentieth century, the South remained overwhelmingly agrarian. It is not surprising, then, that Baptists in the South got a strong reaction from people who could not understand what the better educated and more cultured elite who led the denomination were doing bringing in the "board method" to discharge the mission of the church, whether home or foreign.

Construction of the corporation did not go unchallenged, therefore. Indeed, it met challenge after challenge as rural folk and farmer preachers turned thumbs down on methods and structures they could not document from their Bibles and had serious reservations about on moral grounds. The most notable of the reactions came in the form we know as Landmarkism. Although this controversy split Baptists in the South, an idea for fundraising spawned by the churches' involvement in World War I (1917-1918) began to make the business model look more benign. Selling "War Savings Certificates" and "Liberty Bonds" in the churches led after the war to the "75 Million Campaign" and its successor "The Cooperative Program."

The Southern Baptist Convention took a huge stride forward in its corporate development in 1917 with the creation of an executive committee as "a standing committee of the Convention to act for the body between its sessions."[1] Over the next several years it grew and took on larger responsibilities. In 1926 and 1927 a committee on business efficiency—note the name—assigned the executive committee a wide range of duties and hired its first executive secretary, Austin Crouch (1927-1946).

How thoroughly saturated with the corporation mentality Southern Baptists became by this time is made startlingly clear in a book titled *The Efficient Church*, published in 1923. The author, Gaines S. Dobbins, previously the professor of Sunday School pedagogy, had just assumed a new chair, Professor of Church Efficiency, at the Southern Baptist Theological Seminary in Louisville! In this "study of polity and methods in light of New Testament principles and modern conditions and needs" Dobbins put together a stout argument for interpreting the church as the world's most important business enterprise: "This enterprise, to be sure, is more than a business, but it has its business aspects, and to this extent is subject to the laws that govern business affairs. The application of fundamental efficiency principles in the conduct of the business of a church is of vital importance, and would go far toward bringing in the kingdom of God."[2]

In characteristic Baptist fashion, Dobbins tied the doctrine of efficiency to the New Testament. Jesus himself affirmed it. "'By their fruits ye shall know them' was his test of men and institutions—precisely the test of the modern efficiency expert."[3] The rest of the New Testament followed suit. "The Acts of the Apostles is a manual of church efficiency. . . . The apostle Paul stands out as the world's greatest efficiency expert in religion, and in chapter after chapter of his inspired writings he deals with this practical and vital subject."[4]

Dobbins did show some awareness of the dangers of the business motif. In the Roman Catholic Church it gradually led to a highly efficient hierarchy but one far removed from the "simple, easily understood, efficient polity of the New Testament."[5] Pedobaptist churches, likewise, failed to get back to it. Concern for the corporate model's tendency to go astray notwithstanding, Dobbins proceeded with little hesitation to endorse and applaud the rapidly burgeoning Southern Baptist corporation as having all but achieved the ideal of "efficiency in co-oper-ation." The 75 Million Campaign "demonstrated beyond question the efficiency of the Baptist ideal for co-operative effort."[6]

What Dobbins wanted to see was a more complete infusion of local churches with the ideal of efficiency. "A church is a business enterprise, and must, therefore, meet ordinary requirements of a business institu-tion," he contended. He proceeded to give directions to achieve efficiency in teaching and training, organized service, church management, and enlistment and financial management. He quoted business efficiency expert Roger W. Babson's *Religion and Business* with warm approval when he said that "the church represents the greatest industry in the world today, as well as the oldest. . . . Yet from the business man's point of view this industry is the most indifferently operated of any industry in the world."[7] Dobbins depicted the pastor as an executive and added, "It is of very great consequence that the modern pastor seek to develop the quali-ties of a good executive, that he may have the proper oversight of this immensely important phase of his church life."[8]

A quarter of a century later, Dobbins described efficiency as "an overworked word," but he judged nonetheless that "the ideal which it represents is not outmoded."[9] Indeed, he proceeded to set forth "essen-tials" of both personal and corporate efficiency. "The minister himself must be an efficient person, and he must gather about him efficient per-sons." So, too, the congregation. "A church is an organic body, hence the minister's success as executive will be measured in terms of his grasp and use of the essentials of corporate efficiency."[10] A few years hence, Dobbins published a *vademecum* for ministers titled *The Churchbook*. The word "efficiency" was muted, but the book is replete with materials and methods for creating an efficient corporation.[11] He didn't need to make a case any longer; the Southern Baptist corporation was already in full bloom.

Dobbins related the business model to local congregations. You can see it also in its impact on institutions. Let me cite an expert who spent the bulk of his career at the heart of the corporation, as president of the Sunday School Board of the SBC, James L. Sullivan. This may shock you in its bluntness.

The institution, unlike the Convention, is a corporation. It must operate under a system of management to produce accomplishments for the churches, to fulfill the purposes for which the institution brought it into being. For that reason, an institution is not a democracy. Matters are not to be taken under consideration by employees to see whether they will carry out orders or not. In a corporate structure, like a Southern Baptist institution, the worker must either carry out the directives or seek employment elsewhere. It is just that simple. All democratic processes are taking place in the chart above the executive officer, none below him. Above him the question is "Wilt thou?" Below him the directive is, "Thou shalt." That is the difference between a democratic process and the operation of a corporate structure. For this reason some people are temperamentally unqualified to serve Southern Baptist institutions because they want to work as if the institution were a democracy. Such is impossible for Baptist agencies if the mission of the institution or agency is to be fulfilled.[12]

Gaines Dobbins' "efficient church" has come full circle. If you read Sullivan's statement carefully, you may find yourself in shock at its theological implications. Theologically it says, "The Holy Spirit (which presumably accounts for the church's very existence) operates only above the level of the executive. God personally present has nothing to do with the minds and hearts of persons below that level." Where does the Holy Spirit enter into the life and work of Baptists?

In the Landmarkist view, of course, the Spirit must confine the divine activity to the local congregation since it alone is church. The former president of the Sunday School Board, however, sees decisions, presumably Spirit-guided, above the level of the CEO (chief operating officer). Pressing upward in the corporation, we would come to the Southern Baptist Convention in its annual meeting. Adrian Rogers, twice president of the SBC, gave us the answer by way of a stark if utterly ridiculous analogy: "If we decide that pickles have souls, then those who teach in our seminaries should teach that pickles have souls, or they ought not to take our money."

Business and the Spiritual Life

How did this corporate mentality impact spirituality? In a doctoral study of "Spirituality among Southern Baptist Clergy as Reflected in Selected Autobiographies" for the period 1845 to 1942, Loyd Allen demonstrated the significant changes that redid the whole landscape in Baptist spirituality. Contrary to the impression many people might have, he concluded that "the spirituality of Southern Baptist clergy in 1942 differed from the spirituality of the ministers who had formed the SBC in 1845."[13] How did it differ?

First, a more personal and wholistic model of spirituality witnessed for instance in John Gano, William Hickman, Sr., James Ireland, and John Taylor gave way to "spirituality as negotiation." Whereas earlier Baptist ministers, in the Puritan train, accentuated God's initiative, later ones stressed that Christian life consisted of a series of transactions between the believer and God, the most important of which occurred in conversion. "The spirituality of Southern Baptist clergy was as individualistic as ever," Allen remarked, "but it was less personal and relational. The deal was made between one person and God, but the dynamics were more those of a negotiated contract than a personal relationship."[14]

Concurrent with the shift from a more personal to a more transactional model was a change to more static images of God in which God was expected to deposit grace for those who sought it. God became what Allen calls "the master planner or celestial boss who had devised a program for each believer to follow."[15] As minister W. B. Crumpton put it, "God [had] a program prepared for everyone" and whatever happened was "all a part of the chain of God's great plan."[16] Consequently, the objective was to learn the plan because, if believers did their part, God would do God's.

Not surprisingly, Allen reported, diminishment of a more personal relationship with God led to the "subordination of the traditional means of grace to the goals of the corporate structure of Southern Baptists."[17] Scripture, prayer, worship, and community came to be viewed as objective means by which the Convention could achieve its mission.

Scripture, of course, remained central in Southern Baptist spirituality. The faithful read the Bible, memorized it, and quoted it, but they made less symbolic and affective use than their forebears had. The Bible became more of an objective criterion to measure the spiritual life than "a Spirit-interpreted medium of communication in divine-human encounter," said Allen.[18] Preoccupation with correct interpretation, which entered into the decision to sever ties with the American Baptist Publication Society and establish a Southern Baptist Sunday School Board in 1891 and then, in 1925, to adopt the first *Baptist Faith and Message*, resulted in a divorce from the personal encounter that characterized earlier Baptist spirituality.

Something similar happened in regard to prayer. Whereas early Baptists thought of prayer in much the same intensely personal way Bunyan defined it, after 1891 prayer became more often than not "a tool for intervening with God on behalf of the unsaved" and standardized in wording and tone.[19] Prayer took on an objective quality in the battle to win unbelievers. Unbelievers, minister W. E. Penn wrote, "could not keep those seats and remain unbelievers, for the prayers of Christians would prevail."[20] Most prayers were brief and pointed petitions for spouses, clothes, rain, health, etc., rather than intensely personal communion, communication, or conversation with God. Prayer entailed persistent negotiation!

"Southern Baptist worship moved steadily toward external means to achieve external ends," Allen concluded.[21] The pattern came from revival services, and all aspects of church life—the Sunday school, the preaching, the singing, the gathering—aimed at this objective. Spirituality was assessed also by public professions and contributions.

Given these changes, it is not surprising to see that spiritual guidance through the community of believers decreased also. Allen discerned diminishment in two of the more evident ways in which spiritual guidance occurred in early Baptist spirituality: personal testimony and ongoing discipline.

Personal testimony was still prominent in the early twentieth century both in revivals and in congregations. To save converts from embarrassment of verbalizing their experience, however, Southern Baptist ministers began restricting the hearing of these testimonies to evangelists and pastors. The consequence was, Allen remarked, disengagement of the inquirer's experience from the larger community and turning spiritual guidance over to professional clergy.[22] "I have long ceased to expect an extended and connected story from those seeking membership in the churches. . . .," W. B. Crumpton wrote in 1921. "The process by which they were led to this confession would be interesting, but is not at all necessary."[23] Minister M. P. Hunt wrote that, when he was converted, he had to ask "the privilege of saying a word" to the congregation that had just accepted him in its membership.[24] Community guidance, Allen judged, "had become impersonal and ritualized."[25]

Church discipline experienced a similar slide. Allen suggested two reasons for this: One was a tendency to place more responsibility for the spiritual life of the congregation in the hands of professionals, especially the pastor. The other was diminishment of community as a result of the use of mass evangelism methods.[26] As noted minister J. B. Cranfill remarked, "I never have been strong on turning folks out of the church, feeling as I do somewhat like the Catholic priest who said the Catholics never withdraw fellowship from one of their members except for heresy, their view being that the weaker a man is the more he needs the church."[27] Disappearance of spiritual guidance in the community of believers had more serious consequences. Without it congregations sought unity in objective criteria such as the number of converts and participants and the level of giving.

Whereas early Baptist spirituality was wholistic, Allen found increasing bifurcation of affective and intellectual elements in the autobiographies of ministers in the period after 1891. Although the affective was amply attested in experience of tears, especially as the criterion for genuine religious experience, recording and rational explication of such experiences as dreams virtually vanished. "By 1942 the emotional response of weeping stood alone as a separate and objective criterion for judging the authenticity of conversion," Allen noted. "The more unpredictable dreams and visions had all but disappeared among Southern Baptist clergy."[28] Sacred music, instead, began to carry the burden of affective expression. The result was to move the spirituality "away from a balanced and wholistic model capable of reaching the depths of the personality."[29]

Conversion and call were two other prominent indexes for the dramatic shift in spirituality as Southern Baptists entered the twentieth century.

Conversion retained a central place in talk about religion, Allen concluded, "but personal insight into the authors' own experiences decreased."[30] Before 1845, conversion entailed a lengthy four-stage process:

1. awakening to God's commandments and futile attempt to fulfill them
2. increasing sense of helplessness and recognition that Christ alone could save
3. infusion of saving grace
4. continuing struggle between faith and doubt.[31]

By 1891 this process had come under serious scrutiny, and "conversion became briefer and more transactional."[32] Indeed, emphasis was placed on a one-time transaction rather than the earlier concept of a continuing engagement initiated and sustained by God. In addition, conversion "became part of a mass-production campaign."[33] Evangelists exerted great energy to produce statistics, and the age of baptism dropped significantly, in some cases including children three to five years old. With all of this came a tendency to highlight human rather than divine initiative. Because real conversions frequently did not take place, ministers found alternative experiences that could supply what the earlier ones lacked, that is, "second conversions" and frequently rebaptism. Some, too, emulated Pentecostals in claiming later experiences of the Holy Spirit.

Calling also underwent a change in this period. Some experienced a call to ministry very similar to conversions recorded in an earlier period. Communities of faith entered less into the determination of a vocation than they had earlier. The calling was viewed as a decision negotiated by the individual with God. Allen discerned a four-step pattern in many memoirs after 1891:

1. the call accompanied by assurance
2. delay in performing duty
3. negotiation
4. reassurance and continuing active ministry.[34]

Regarding the negotiation, Allen commented, "The spirituality underlying the pattern of call to ministry in these examples was more forensic and contractual than personal. The inner persuasion of the Holy Spirit in direct relationship with the believer was often subordinated to a negotiated settlement according to objective signs from a distant God."[35] Finally, Allen noted, the spirituality of Southern Baptist ministers sought validation of piety in denominational activities rather than, as before 1845, in creative action in the world as a sign of obedience to God. The ultimate test was winning converts. As long-time minister B. J. W. Graham phrased it, "The greatest thing in the world is to lead a lost soul to Christ."[36]

Whereas earlier Baptists viewed the test in terms of introducing people to heart religion manifest in transformed life, now they sought to get commitment to a static contract assuring entrance into heaven. No longer a marginal people in the South, they lacked the powerful motive their forebears had to change society's values. Consequently, Allen concluded, they substituted "objective institutional goals for the ongoing obedient servanthood of former days."[37]

The prevailing model in society, that of business, shaped not only the developing organization of the SBC but also Southern Baptist spirituality. Just as earnings served as the criterion for business success, so too did money raised to meet the churches' needs determine the level of piety. As M. P. Hunt put it, "I have never seen a greater manifestation of love for Christ than was exhibited in their giving during the collection."[38] Allen observed here how the autobiographies of this later period differed from earlier ones.

In earlier Southern Baptist autobiographies most of the space is given to descriptions of the authors' religious experiences and how those affected their ministerial work. By far the predominant themes were the writer's own conversion experience and call to ministry. After 1891 the balance shifted. The subject written most about in the lives published between 1891 and 1942 was work done in positions that had as their main function fundraising and disbursement. The favorite theme of Southern Baptist clergy in the first half of the twentieth century was how to raise and spend money.[39] Allen concluded that "the applied spirituality of Baptists had become a spirituality of *busy-ness*."[40]

Why did a more personal and wholistic spirituality manifesting itself in concern for transformation of persons and society end up in such a static concept of conversion as a one-time transaction negotiated between the individual and God that tested itself by institutional involvement and busyness? Loyd Allen cited three factors that blend into one another.

1. Baptists in the South lost their marginal status.
2. Caught up with their own success, Baptists relied increasingly on methods of mass revivalism.
3. Coming of age, as it were, as the business model replaced earlier social models, Baptists bought into the business model lock, stock, and barrel.

Today's Supermarket

The approach to spirituality I see among Baptists today probably is best described as seeker. Indeed, sociologist Wade Clark Roof has labeled the so-called Baby Boomers, persons born between 1946 and 1965, "a generation of seekers," and he has contended that they are "altering the religious landscape of America in the 1990s."[41] Boomers vary substantially among themselves, but they share three basic characteristics:

1. They emphasize inner lives but also outward commitment.
2. They no longer speak of covenant, but they mesh their personal stories with their larger commitments.
3. They place much emphasis on the value of "spirit" over institution; that is, they value a subjective approach to religion.

In writing about Baptist approaches to spirituality from a historical perspective, I am intrigued by the fact that Baptists came into being with another generation of "seekers" in the seventeenth century. Many early Baptists, including Roger Williams, described themselves as "seekers." Like many other Puritans, they wanted to know God and they did not have much confidence in the guidance offered in the dominant churches of their day. They kept their agendas open and tried out the wide range of religious offerings, hoping they would find the one that best met their outlook and need. I find many Baptists, not just Baby Boomers but especially their successors, the "GenXers," doing the same thing today. Consequently you will probably find people called Baptists shopping in a supermarket of spiritual wares.

Richard Foster has singled out six traditions that appeal to many Baptists and also to persons of other backgrounds.

1. The *contemplative* tradition emphasizes "the prayer-filled life." Its most fundamental characteristics and movements, Foster says, are love, peace, delight, emptiness or darkness, fire, wisdom, and transformation. Its strengths include fanning the flames of love of God and neighbor, insistence that head religion alone is inadequate, accentuation of the importance of prayer, and valuing of the solitary way. Yet it has some weaknesses: a tendency to separate itself from everyday life, a kind of "consuming asceticism" that leads to excesses, a tendency to devalue intellectual efforts to articulate faith, and an inclination to denigrate the importance of the community of faith.

2. The *holiness* tradition concentrates on the reformation of life and the development of virtuous habits. Exemplified especially by the Methodist

movement, James in the New Testament, and, in more recent days, Dietrich Bonhoeffer, among its strengths are its goal of "an ever deeper formation of the inner personality so as to reflect the glory and goodness of God,"[42] an intentional focus on the heart as the wellspring of action, the hope it gives regarding progress in transformation of character, and "its tough-minded, down-to-earth, practical understanding" of how we grow in grace.[43] There are potential dangers, however, in legalism, Pelagian "works-righteousness," and perfectionism.

3. The *charismatic* tradition centers on discovery of the Spirit-empowered life. Exhibited in Francis of Assisi, the Apostle Paul, and modern Pentecostalism as well as the charismatic movement, it has positive qualities in "an ongoing correction to our impulse to domesticate God," its "constant rebuke to our anemic practice," the continuing challenge it offers to spiritual growth, and the way it gifts and empowers people for witness and service.[44] Dangers are evident, however, in trivialization by focus on external phenomena, in rejection of the rational and intellectual, in divorcing the gifts from the fruit of the Spirit, and in linking the Christian walk to highly speculative scenarios of the end-time.

4. The *social justice* tradition concerns itself especially with the compassionate life. Powerfully attested in the American Quaker saint John Woolman (1720-1772), the eighth century B.C. prophet Amos, and twentieth-century founder of the Catholic Worker, Dorothy Day (1897-1980), Foster observes, it highlights three great themes: compassionate justice (*mishpat*), loving kindness (*hesed*), and peace (*shalom).* Admirable qualities of this tradition are its constant summons to right ordering of society, its enhancement of our understanding of the church, its concern to provide a bridge between personal ethics and social ethics, the way it makes talk about love relevant and forceful, the foundation it provides for ecological concerns, and its holding before us "the relevance of the impossible ideal."[45] Yet it also presents perils: the tendency of social justice to become an end in itself, strident legalism, and too close identification with a particular political agenda.

5. The *evangelical* tradition has to do with the Word-centered life. Visible, according to Foster, in Augustine (354-430), the Apostle Peter, and Billy Graham, this tradition lives for the faithful preaching of the gospel, the

centrality of scriptures as the gospel's repository, and "the confessional witness of the early Christian community as a faithful interpretation of the gospel."[46] Its strengths consist of its fervent call to conversion, its stress upon Jesus' mandate to disciple the nations, its fidelity to the Bible, and its concern for sound doctrine. With these, however, arise some dangers: "a fixation upon peripheral and nonessential matters,"[47] inclination toward a sectarian mentality, "a tendency to present too limited a view of the salvation that is found in Jesus Christ," and bibliolatry.[48]

6. The *incarnational* tradition revolves around the sacramental life. Witnessed in Susanna Wesley (1669-1742), Ark of the Covenant crafter Bezalel (Exod. 31:1-5), and Dag Hammarskjöld (1905-1961), the tradition links experience of God through material media and elevates the liturgy and sacraments not only in the religious sphere but also in everyday life. Foster finds numerous positives in this tradition: its underscoring God's presence in all aspects of our earthly existence, the way it "roots us in everyday life,"[49] how it makes work meaningful, the corrective it offers to Gnostic dualism, its constant beckoning Godward, its emphasis on the body as the means through which we daily experience God, and its deepening of ecological sensitivities. Nevertheless, he points to two special perils, among many: idolatry and seeking "to manage God through externals."[50]

In an "Afterword" Foster speaks optimistically about a "flowing together" of these six streams "into a mighty movement of the Spirit."[51] Although evidence for that seems to me quite limited, I can cite specific examples of both Baptist individuals and Baptist groups attracted to one or another of these six approaches. As a matter of fact, in an article on "Trends in Baptist Spirituality," I have remarked after agreeing with Molly Marshall's list of four (conversionist, charismatic, crusading or prophetic, and contemplative): "We could probably add secular, oriental or quasi-oriental, New Age, plus the prevailing spirituality of various religious bodies (Orthodox, Reformed, Methodist, etc.) and Roman Catholic religious orders (Ignatian, Carmelite, Franciscan, Dominican, etc.)."[52] It's seeker time.

Notes

[1] The fuller story of this development is told by Albert McClellan, *The Executive Committee of the Southern Baptist Convention, 1917-1984* (Nashville: Broadman Press, 1985).

[2] Gaines S. Dobbins, *The Efficient Church* (Nashville: Sunday School Board of the Southern Baptist Convention, 1923), 11-12.

[3] Ibid., 25.

[4] Ibid., 26.

[5] Ibid., 60.

[6] Ibid., 87.

[7] Ibid., 161.

[8] Ibid., 164.

[9] Gaines S. Dobbins, *Building Better Churches: A Guide to Pastoral Ministry* (Nashville: Broadman Press, 1947), 399.

[10] Ibid., 401.

[11] Gaines S. Dobbins, *The Churchbook: A Treasury of Materials and Methods* (Nashville: Broadman Press, 1960).

[12] James L. Sullivan, *Baptist Polity as I See It* (Nashville: Broadman Press, 1983), 172-173.

[13] William Loyd Allen, "Spirituality among Southern Baptist Clergy as Reflected in Selected Autobiographies," Unpublished Ph.D. Dissertation, The Southern Baptist Theological Seminary, Louisville, Kentucky, 1984, 199. Allen grouped the autobiographies into three periods: (1) prior to 1845—John Gano, William Hickman, Sr., James Ireland, and John Taylor; (2) 1845-1891—John Leland Dagg, Z. N. Morrell, Jeremiah Bell Jeter, Johnson Olive, J. M. Pendleton, Thomas C. Teasdale, and William R. Wigginton; and (3) 1891-1942—Sanford Miller Brown, James Britton Cranfill, Washington Bryan Crumpton, George William Gardner, Balus Joseph Winzer Graham, William E. Hatcher, Adoniram Judson Holt, Marion Palmer Hunt, John Lipscomb Johnson, W. E. Penn, and William Thomas Tardy.

[14] Ibid., 161.

[15] Ibid.

[16] Washington Bryan Crumpton, *A Book of Memories, 1842-1920* (Montgomery, AL: Baptist Mission Board, 1921), xi, 37.

[17] Allen, "Spirituality," 163.

[18] Ibid., 165.

[19] Ibid., 167.

[20] W. E. Penn, *The Life and Labors of W. E. Penn the Texas Evangelist* (St. Louis: C. B. Woodward, 1896), 112f.

[21] Allen, "Spirituality," 171.

[22] Ibid., 174.

[23] Crumpton, *A Book of Memories*, 19f.

[24] Marion Palmer Hunt, *The Story of My Life* (Louisville, KY: Herald Press, 1941), 17.

[25] Allen, "Spirituality," 175.

[26] Ibid., 176.

[27] James Britton Cranfill, *From Memory: Reminiscences, Recitals, and Gleanings from a Bustling and Busy Life* (Nashville: Broadman Press, 1937), 107.

[28] Allen, "Spirituality," 180.

[29] Ibid., 181.

[30] Ibid.

31 Ibid., citing Bill J. Leonard, "Getting Saved in America: Conversion Event in a Pluralistic Culture," The Southern Baptist Theological Seminary, Louisville, Kentucky, May 4, 1983.

32 Allen, "Spirituality," 182.

33 Ibid., 184.

34 Ibid., 189.

35 Ibid., 191f.

36 B. J. W. Graham, *A Ministry of Fifty Years* (1938), 12.

37 Allen, "Spirituality," 193.

38 Hunt, *The Story of My Life*, 36.

39 Allen, "Spirituality," 196.

40 Ibid.

41 Wade Clark Roof, *A Generation of Seekers: The Spirituality of Baby Boomers* (San Francisco: Harper/Collins, 1992), 1.

42 Richard J. Foster, *Streams of Living Water: Celebrating the Great Traditions of Christian Faith* (HarperSanFrancisco, 1998), 85.

43 Ibid., 88.

44 Ibid., 129.

45 Ibid., 178.

46 Ibid., 219.

47 Ibid., 228.

48 Ibid., 230.

49 Ibid., 267.

50 Ibid., 268.

51 Ibid., 273.

52 E. Glenn Hinson, "Trends in Baptist Spirituality," *Christian Spirituality Bulletin*, 7 (Fall/Winter 1999), 3. Molly Marshall, "The Changing Face of Baptist Discipleship," *Review & Expositor* 95 (Winter 1998), 67-70.

Part 5

A Vision for Baptist Spiritual Formation
Recovering Attentiveness to God

I initially set forth a vision for spiritual formation of Baptists at a CBF assembly in Washington, D.C., June 27, 2007. I was more than a little overwhelmed at the assigned subject: "God, what is your yearning/desire for spiritual formation in the CBF?" Although I have spent much time over many years trying to tell Baptists where to go, I'm a bit hesitant to claim that I can say where it is God is trying to tell us to go. I pray that my years of reflection will come out on somewhat the same road God yearns for all persons, specifically all Christians, to travel.

I hope you will not be disappointed when you do not hear anything new in what I say in this final section. Quite to the contrary, my basic thesis will be that God wants us to do everything we can to help people learn how to live contemplatively in an age and culture far removed from contemplation. Indeed, we should do our best to help a whole society, afflicted with a deep malaise, experience the transformation that only the love of God can effect. To a considerable degree, what I want to say is that the way forward is to recover the contemplative tradition with which we Baptists began.

It may have surprised some of you to hear me identify Baptists with the contemplative tradition, for that tradition is usually associated with monasticism. Those who have been my students and who have read my writings, however, should not be surprised, for I have expended much effort to demonstrate how our Baptist/Puritan forebears showed surprising similarities to medieval contemplatives in their spirituality. They did so because they deliberately returned to those sources in order to learn how to achieve their goal of a "further reformation"—heart religion manifested in transformed lives and the transformation of society.[1]

Recover?

You will notice that I used the word "recover" when I spoke about the contemplative tradition. The reason I did that is because in four centuries of our Baptist pilgrimage the contemplative tradition, which focuses especially on the transformation that God can work in us, has taken some heavy hits.[2] As I have interpreted them in the preceding sections, major changes have come in three phases:

1. A *conversionist* phase in the "Great Awakening" and frontier revival
2. A *pragmatist* phase as Baptists in America grew up during the period when the business model imposed itself on all aspects of American life
3. A *seeker* phase as America has become the most pluralistic society on earth.[3]

We can find positive and admirable aspects in each of these phases, but they have also created some challenges to the whole-personed spiritual formation that our covenant with God should entail.

The conversionist phase freed Baptists from the crippling grip of hyper-Calvinism and enabled us to pursue the Great Commission, but it also launched a shift from a lifelong process of spiritual formation to the front end of the process. Winning converts shoved aside the concern for formation throughout life. The result was too many newborn Baptists who failed to grow into adult Christians.

The pragmatist phase harnessed an energy and sometimes useful ideas found in the burgeoning business industry in America, but it swallowed hook, line, and sinker, too, the success motif with its accent on marketing that motivated business and made our relationship with God a matter of negotiation rather than intimacy. The key thing became faith as a business deal carefully confirmed rather than faith as growing in the covenant with God.

The seeker phase has opened up many options, especially in encounters with other cultures and religions, during a period of deepened religious search, but it has also created the problem of overchoice. Up to the Civil War, America was an overwhelmingly Protestant nation. From the 1860s to the 1960s, it was a Protestant/Catholic nation. Since that time, it has become a multi-religious nation. How do we select from so many options what will contribute to a healthy growth in our relationship with God and with one another?

My answer to that question is not "Go West, young man!" or "Go East!" or "Go North!" or "Go South!" but "Go back!" We had best hitch up our britches and wade back down our Baptist stream to where it meets the Puritan stream, then down the Puritan stream to where it meets the Anglican stream, and then down the Anglican stream to where it meets the Catholic mainstream, and then down the Catholic mainstream to where it flows out of the Jewish spring we have come to know in and through Jesus of Nazareth.

Baptists have often spoken disparagingly of "tradition," but I would like to underscore here a positive meaning. Convention is the external, the husk, and we can discard a lot of conventions. Tradition is the essence, the kernel, and we cannot dispense with it. Permit me, then, to lay out some of the essentials of the contemplative tradition that I think God desires for Baptists in our age to recover.

The Covenant

I begin with the covenant at the heart of our relationship with God. On the American frontier, Baptists pushed the covenant aside in their debates with groups who based their practice of baptizing infants on it, but we cannot develop a healthy spirituality without restoring the idea of covenant to the center of our thinking and practice.

In the Abrahamic tradition of faith the eternal God out of love chose to effect a covenant between God's self and humankind. What God has yearned for from eternity is that humans will seek to enter ever more deeply into this covenant relationship both individually and corporately.

From ancient times Jews and Christians, including Baptists, have drawn on the analogy of marriage and invoked the love tryst of the Song of Songs to enable their constituents to understand how intimate our relationship with God should be. You see, this covenant is not an over/under, master/slave, liege lord/serf kind of relationship. By God's choice it is a lover/beloved, spouse/spouse, parent/child kind of relationship. As Paul reminded the Romans, "You did not receive a spirit of servitude to come groveling in fear, but you received a spirit of adoption as children in which we cry out, '*Abba*, Father!'" (Rom. 8:15, my paraphrase).

You hear the terms of this covenant clearly laid out in the two great commandments: "You shall love the Lord your God with all your heart, soul, mind, and strength" and "You shall love your neighbor as yourself" (Mark 12:30-31, Matt. 22:37-39, Luke 10:27). If Jesus taught us anything, he taught us this: We must keep our focus in spiritual formation always on the fact that the eternal God of infinite love has fallen in love with us and wants us to love God back with our whole being and to love every human in the way God loves us. As H. Richard Niebuhr stated superbly, the purpose of the church and its ministry is "the increase among men [and women] of the love of God and of neighbor."[4] That surely is what God yearns for spiritual formation among Baptists today.

How will we grow in the love of God and of neighbor? Did Jesus not give us the answer to that question in Matthew 6:33? To the anxiety-ridden of his day, he said, "Seek first God's mysterious presence and God's okaying of you; then these other things will fall into place" (Matt. 6:33, my paraphrase). Please note that I am not adopting the NRSV version, "Strive first for the kingdom." Striving only adds to anxiety. We must recognize that we grow in the love of God not by striving, but by surrender. We all have within us a "homing instinct," like that of the pigeon that takes it to the place of its birth, but even as we seek God, God is seeking us. We would have no hope in this covenant relationship were that not true.

The "kingdom" is not a certain type of society or government. As Jesus illustrated it, the kingdom is mysterious, like yeast in the lump of dough (Matt. 13:33=Luke 13:21), a mustard seed (Matt. 13:31, Mark 4:31, Luke 13:19), a crop growing of its own accord (Mark 4:28), or a thief in the night (Matt. 24:43, Luke 12:39). In Matthew's Gospel, "righteousness" is God's work of transformation—good trees bearing good fruit (Matt. 7:17-18; Luke 6:43), not those who say "Lord, Lord," but those who do the will of God (Matt. 7:21-22), and the downright good who feed the hungry, give drink to the thirsty, clothe the naked, and give hospitality to strangers without even thinking about it (Matt. 25:31-46).

Paul's prayer for the Philippians should be our constant prayer: "that God's love in you may grow more and more in understanding and in every sensitivity so that you may have a sense of things that really matter, in order that you may be pure and without reproach in the day of Christ,

64

filled with fruit of righteousness that rebounds through Jesus Christ to the glory and praise of God."

We need to open to the love of God like flowers opening to the morning sun. God is Love. God's love energies brought our world into being. Those love energies sustain our world and direct it toward some meaningful end. And, just as the sun's rays constantly bathe our earth, those same love energies are always pouring on us. But *we* have to open, for God does not drive a bulldozer.

Learning to open to the transforming love of God has been the concern of the contemplative tradition from ancient times on, and, insofar as we can do anything to facilitate our growth in the love of God, opening is our single-minded concern.

Opening

I make it sound very easy, very simple—"Just open!" But you and I know that it isn't easy or simple. We've experienced storms in life that have caused us to pull our shutters to and to close our doors and bar them from the inside. I'm not speaking so much about physical storms—though they certainly cause such reactions—but about psychic, emotional, and spiritual storms. You love someone. That person exploits, twists, distorts, or abuses your love, and you pull back. Thenceforward, you fear opening again lest you suffer a similar experience.

My mother did something for me that has made it hard to open. As I grew up in poverty in the Missouri Ozarks during the Great Depression, she drilled into me that I was never to take anything free. "If you don't take anything you don't earn or merit, you won't be owing anybody anything. You'll have your pride."

"Pride" underscored! In some ways that was a gift, and I know some people who could use my mother's advice. But my mother also left me with a problem: that of accepting grace. I don't think I accepted a piece of candy from another person until I was twenty-five years of age. I would always say, "No, thank you. I'm about to have lunch," or "I just had some," or (the real reason) "My mother would skin me."

George Herbert, the great Anglican poet and pastor, fingered the universal human dilemma exactly as he drew his classic poem "The Temple" to its dramatic close. You know these lines:

Love bade me welcome: yet my soul drew back,
  Guilty of dust and sin.
But quick-eyed Love, observing me grow slack
  From my first entrance in,
Drew nearer to me, sweetly questioning,
  If I lack'd anything.

A guest, I answer'd, worthy to be here:
  Love said, You shall be he.
I the unkind, ungrateful? Ah, my dear,
  I cannot look on thee.
Love took my hand, and smiling did reply,
  Who made the eyes but I?[5]

So it isn't easy to open. Yet, with God's gentle wooing, we must, from the inside. God is not a bulldozer. God will not break our door down. We have to open. What can we do to open ourselves and to help other people to open themselves to the transforming love of God?

The School of Love

Bernard of Clairvaux spoke about the monastery as *schola dilectionis* or *schola caritatis,* "the school of love." We can learn much from the Benedictine tradition about how such schools may open people to the transforming love of God, above all, through prayer. In our active lives we won't be able to imitate the full regimen set out by the Rule of St. Benedict and practiced today in Cistercian monasteries. But could we not find some way to siphon some insights from the whole regimen and from each of these elements?

Many people have found Thomas Merton's observation about the contemplative life very true. The contemplative life in the strictest sense is led in monasteries, he said. "But in a broader sense every life can be dedicated to some extent to contemplation, and even the most active of lives can and should be balanced by a contemplative element—leavened by the peace and order and clarity that can be provided by meditation, interior prayer, and the deep penetration of the most fundamental truths of human existence."[8]

What about the three chief elements of the Benedictine regimen?

Psalmody has virtually disappeared from Baptist usage, but Baptist and other hymnals contain hymnic adaptations of Psalms, and one hears scores of praise hymns, many of which are Psalms. GenXers, in particular, relate to life through music. Music has great power to form people spiritually. Why not the Psalms?

Lectio divina, the soul of monastic contemplative formation, is probably the easiest for a people as biblicistic as Baptists to take to. We share with contemplatives through the ages the conviction that God speaks to us, above all, through these sacred writings. Benedictines used *lectio divina* to outline four steps on the way to developing intimacy in one's relationship to God:

1. *Lectio* means reading and mulling over scripture texts like a cow chewing the cud. Teresa of Ávila described this as lifting up water out of a cistern with a bucket. It is hard but necessary work. Merton called it the "front porch" of prayer.
2. *Meditatio* takes you from head to heart. Here God helps more. Teresa called this "the prayer of quiet" and suggested that it is like water being lifted by a water wheel.
3. *Oratio* involves direct conversation, communication, and communion with God. At this level, Teresa said, "the waters of grace have risen to the neck of the soul," like water flowing through a stream.
4. *Contemplatio* has to do with "resting in God." We have arrived at our goal. It is like rain falling, Teresa said.

Spending time in silence may pose the greatest challenge in this era whose chief symbol may well be the Internet, a cell phone, an iPod, a television blaring when no one is in the room, or other noise box. Here we may have to do what Jesus often did and what monks have done in imitation of him, that is, fast from these distracting media and retreat to the desert to spend time in solitude and silence. Churches could make retreats for all of their members a major responsibility.

At first glance the obvious differences between a monastery and a church might seem to make even the thought ludicrous. A monastery is an intimate community of intensely dedicated persons who try to find God's will for their lives. Cloistered monasteries, such as Bernard spoke about, shut out many of the world's distractions. They eliminate sounds and sights that get in the way of their main objective: to fulfill the two great commandments, love of God and love of neighbor. They also structure a regimen that may assure spiritual growth difficult to attain in the world: about three or four hours of the *Opus Dei*, three or four of *Lectio Divina*, and six hours of labor in silence.

Those are valid points. A little time spent in a monastery, however, might temper some of the artificial distinctions you visualize between the monastery and the "world" and between monks and the people of the "world," as it did for Thomas Merton. The word "school" is helpful here, for it suggests continuous seeking and learning—not perfection.

Within our Baptist context, however, we are not likely soon to see monasteries develop, so we must look at other social models in which we may develop "schools of love" through which we can effect the transformation of individual lives and, from thence, society. The dominant model in America, and perhaps much of the western world today, is that of the business corporation. In a provocative book titled *Soul at Work: Spiritual Leadership in Organizations*, Margaret Benefiel, a Quaker, shows how spirituality can play a role in what happens in business organizations, even churchly ones, but she is talking about something that is happening in a few instances, not on a wide scale.[7]

Puritans, including early Baptists, focused on the family unit.[8] Quite a lot of schooling in the love of God and of others should happen there today, too, but we must recognize a serious change in the nature and role of families in America. We might think of modular families in which people could be formed in love. Thomas Merton once adapted the Cistercian model for a group of families and individuals who lived near Gethsemani; they called themselves "The Families of St. Benedict." I don't know how long the experiment lasted.

Churches should provide the major venue for a "school of love." Most of us will recognize, however, that most such schools will consist of those who elect to enroll in them. Programs such as the Upper Room's *Companions in Christ*, now adapted even for spiritual formation of children, point the way, and it is quite commendable that CBF has undertaken to promote it. The Academy for Spiritual Formation may come the closest in its deliberate design to a school of love.

Although a monastic community might be a sort of graduate-level school of love, the Apostle Paul seems to have envisioned churches as schools of love when he wrote his letters to the Corinthians and to the Romans. He didn't know the Roman congregations firsthand, but he did have intimate acquaintance with the fractious Corinthians. In

1 Corinthians 13 and in Romans 12 he cited particulars of love in deed that, God helping, would enable a far-from-perfect human family to experience unity and community, its faults notwithstanding.

Paul thought about these early communities of faith as families, though somewhat more complex than the natural families we know in our society. They included not only parents and children, but also slaves who may also have had children. You can easily imagine how complex relationships became in such households. Multiply the complexity many times, and you will see what a church family looked like. Yet it was such a diverse and fragile family that Paul thought should be a school of love.

I don't have a tidy program, starting with leaders, for effecting the transformation of churches into schools of love, but Douglas Steere, one of the eminent Quakers of the last half of the twentieth century, latched onto a formula for ministry that I have seen do exactly that in a Petersburg, Virginia, church I served as interim pastor. Although I'm confident that he practiced this ministry before, he got a descriptive phrase for it from the brilliant Jewish philosopher Martin Buber. In a Friends' meeting at Haverford College in 1951 Buber said, "The greatest thing one can do for another is to confirm what is deepest in another." Douglas Steere made confirming "what is deepest in another" the object of his life and ministry.

I think that comes very close to what Jesus made the object of his life and ministry. It flashes like a neon sign in the Zacchaeus story preserved for us by Saint Luke (19:1-10). In it Jesus models four facets of confirmation:

1. attention
2. acceptance
3. association
4. affirmation

In this dramatic episode he gives us some insight into the art of loving not only those who reciprocate our love, but also those who many despise, scorn, and ostracize.

Tax collectors are not popular in our society, where they work for us, the American people. Imagine how a people living under the Roman yoke felt about one of their own who worked not for them but for the oppressor collecting taxes, and had gotten rich skimming a little extra for himself. Not only so, this particular tax collector presented a comic spectacle when he tried to get a look at Jesus as the popular teacher walked through Jericho surrounded by an adoring throng. Too short to see over the onlookers, he had to jump up and down on tiptoes. Like many small people, however, he was canny. Seeing Jesus head toward a sycamore tree hanging over a Jericho road, Zacchaeus hurried ahead and squirreled up the tree so he could look down at Jesus as he passed by. That bold move opened the way for Jesus to confirm what was deepest in Zacchaeus.

"When he came to that place," says Luke, "he stopped and looked up." This despised little wretch surely expected Jesus to look any which way but up. If he gave him a look, it would be the withering one so many others cast his way. But Jesus gave him a precious gift: attention. Inattention hurts. It hurts worse than being badly treated, and we humans can't stand a lot of inattention. It saps self-esteem. It shrivels our souls. When Jesus looked up, old Zach must almost have fallen out of that tree.

To attention, Jesus added acceptance. "Zacchaeus, hurry and get down from there, for I have to stay at your house today." In ten seconds Jesus had confirmed him with the precious gifts of attention and acceptance. If you have ever experienced ostracism, an iceberg treatment, like Zacchaeus received day after day, you can sense the added confirmation that would come from Jesus risking his life and reputation by association. A nobody became somebody! His heart must have been thumping 150 times a minute. Luke says, "He scrambled down and received him rejoicing!"

To attention and acceptance certified in association, Jesus added a fourth incalculable element in confirmation: affirmation. No sooner had he gotten Jesus into the house than old Zach felt compelled to put the best face on himself and his activities. "See, sir, I give half of everything I possess to the poor, and if I have ripped anybody off, I repay fourfold" (Luke 19:8).

People who are despised and rejected feel they need to justify themselves. This confession may mislead us to attribute Jesus' next action to Zacchaeus' good deeds, but the parable of the Pharisee and the tax collector (Luke 18:9-14) would negate that. Not as a consequence of any worthiness in this tax collector, but on the basis of God's infinite mercy and love, Jesus declared, "Today salvation has come to this house, for he, too is a child of Abraham" (Luke 19:9).

As schools of love, churches can create a culture of confirming what is deepest in others by attention, acceptance, association, and affirmation. Want to try it?

Contemplation in a World of Action

Millions of Americans, including many Baptists, will doubtless dispute the value of contemplation in a world caught up in activity for activity's sake, quick to invent distractions, and uncomfortable with even a moment's silence. They still think like most of the seventy-five students I took to the Abbey of Gethsemani in 1960.

To be honest, I didn't take them to Gethsemani to learn about contemplation or to meet Thomas Merton, but to learn about the Middle Ages. Merton was our bonus. After he had talked to us about life in the monastery, he asked if we had questions.

One student asked what I feared one would ask: "What is a smart fellow like you doing throwing his life away in a place like this?"

I waited for Merton to open his mouth and eat that guy alive. But he didn't. He chuckled and said something that bowled me over: "I am here because I believe in prayer. That is my vocation."

You could have knocked me over with a feather. I had never met anyone who believed in prayer enough to think of it as a vocation. All the way back to the seminary that afternoon, those words kept echoing in my head alongside the Protestant rubric, "God has no hands but our hands, no feet but our feet, no voice but our voice." I began to pray that Merton might be right, for, if everything depends on us, our world is in a desperate, a hopeless condition.

I must confess here that I didn't really begin to grasp what Thomas Merton was all about until after his untimely death in 1968. I scanned the manuals he put together to teach novices, which he sent me, and read *Spiritual Direction and Meditation*, the first book he gave me, but all of that rolled off like water off of a duck's back. After his death, however, I received invitations to speak about him that necessitated that I read all of his published works.

Little by little, I began to discern Merton's message for our day, the dire necessity of contemplation for a world of action, a world that no longer accorded time and made room to seek wisdom for its own sake, to seek God. As he put behind him the negative view of the "world" he brought to Gethsemani in 1941, during the late 1950s and 1960s he sought to show how contemplation could lead to more purposeful action. So much of our action in today's world, Merton insisted, is purposeless because it does not proceed from authentic being. "He who attempts to act and do things for others or for the world without deepening his own self-understanding, freedom, integrity and capacity to love, will not have anything to give others. He will communicate to them nothing but the contagion of his own obsessions, his aggressiveness, his ego-centered ambitions, his delusions about ends and means, his doctrinaire prejudices and ideas."[9]

I think Thomas Merton has answered the question about God's yearning with which I began, not for Baptists but for all Christians. What he did was to take the wisdom of the whole contemplative tradition and address its insights to what he described as "an illusory and deceptive world of collective unreason."

In a work titled *The Inner Experience*, which he wrote initially in 1959 and edited several times but that was not published until 2003, Merton sought to prescribe a contemplative solution to our modern dilemma:

We are selves fragmented by our environment with its many distractions and need reintegration as unified human persons. In order to become whole, we must strip away our false, exterior selves and discover and awaken our inner selves. Western culture today works against the spontaneous development and discovery of these inner selves. We can prepare ourselves to receive grace, but we do not possess in ourselves the ability to discover and awaken them, for we will find our true selves only when we find God. "Since our inmost 'I' is the perfect image of God, then when that 'I' awakens, he finds within himself the Presence of Him Whose image he is. And, by a paradox beyond all human expressions, God and the soul seem to have but one single 'I.' They are (by divine grace) as though one single person. They breathe and live and act as one."[10]

Recovery of wholeness will not mean isolation from the world. Quite to the contrary, it should lead our inner selves to see the world from what Merton called "a deeper and more spiritual viewpoint"[11]—a child's rather than a lumberman's view of a tree! A Christian contemplative is not merely "alone with the Alone," but, inseparable from Christ, is one with "all the other 'I's' who live in Christ."[12] He continued: "The life of contemplation is, then, not simply a life of human technique and discipline; it is the life of the Holy Spirit in our souls. The whole duty of the contemplative is to abandon what is base and trivial in his life, and do all he can to conform himself to the secret and obscure promptings of the Spirit of God."[13]

An Ecumenical Endeavor

I cannot close without underscoring the importance of working together not only with other Christians, but also with persons of other faiths in an age that will require the united effort of all humans possibly even to survive. As the preceding paragraph hints, the mature Merton constantly expanded his understanding of the word "catholic" and envisioned a "quite momentous" role that contemplatives might play in interfaith dialogue and cooperation.[14] I doubt whether I need to remind you how critical it is to cultivate interfaith connections that might ease tensions between Christians, Jews, and Muslims.

First, let me express thanks to United Methodists and to God for the development of a serious cooperation between CBF and the United Methodist Church through the Upper Room. Some of you have participated in the training session for *Companions in Christ*, and quite a few have attended the Academy for Spiritual Formation and read and contributed to *Weavings*. We do not need to reinvent Baptist versions of ideas and programs that work quite well. We need each other. It is far better for us to share labors with those whose understanding of "evangelical" is so close to ours than to carry on a pitched battle with people only nominally Baptist who think they know more than God does.

Second, I think God offers hearty approval of ties we establish with other Christian bodies in the area of spiritual formation. Perhaps you will forgive a little prejudice on my part, but the Roman Catholic Church has unmatched wealth in its many religious orders and the contemplative tradition it shares unreservedly. I thank God every morning for Pope John XXIII daring to throw open the windows and doors of the Church, to start calling us "separated brothers," and to launch a new epoch in church history. Thanks to John's "New Pentecost," we've become co-laborers rather than competitors with Episcopalians, Presbyterians, Quakers, Disciples, Orthodox, and most other Christian religious bodies—save our fellow Baptists in the South—as we traipse through our contemplative stream toward the mainstream.

Perhaps you can chalk this up to my age (eighty-one as of last July 27), but I would plead that we not limit our listening and learning to other Christians. God, whom we have come to know in and through Jesus of Nazareth, a Jew, is not of such limited candlepower that God can only illuminate Baptists or Protestants or Catholics or Orthodox or those who name the name of Christ. The universal Christ, who said, "I am the way, the truth, and the life," is not one whom missionaries "take" throughout the whole wide earth. A Christ they can "take" isn't big enough to help anyone. No, the universal Christ will meet them wherever they go—in every culture and in every religion, wherever truth is. We need not apologize to say that we wished others would know God through Jesus Christ as we do, but we Christians must not say they have no light. Just as Merton reminded my students, "we are all beginners" when it comes to knowing God.

Summary and Conclusion

What is God's yearning for spiritual formation among Baptists, then? I would not want to claim inerrancy and infallibility in my discernment, but I think it boils down to this:

God yearns for us to form everywhere and in every way we can schools of love that will enable those who enroll to open to the transforming love of God, so that they may have a sense of things that really matter, in order that they may become pure in heart and filled with the fruit of the Spirit: love, joy, peace, patience, kindness, goodness, faithfulness, gentleness, self-control. The curriculum for such "schools" would derive from appropriation and adaptation of the centuries of insight accumulated by the contemplative tradition about deepening the covenant between God and ourselves. A practicum would enable students to discover how a contemplative life informs and influences everyday endeavor. Because attentiveness is at the heart of the contemplative life, every effort would be made to listen to and learn from other persons and groups engaged in the same endeavor.

Notes

[1] With apologies for some immodesty in citing my own writings, I would direct you to E. Glenn Hinson, "Southern Baptist and Medieval Spirituality: Surprising Similarities," *Cistercian Studies* 20 (1985), 224-36, and "The Contemplative Roots of Baptist Spirituality," in *Ties that Bind: Life Together in the Baptist Vision*, ed. Gary Furr and Curtis W. Freeman (Macon, GA: Smyth & Helwys, 1994), 69-82.

[2] See my lengthy article sketching these developments titled "Baptist Approaches to Spirituality," *Baptist History & Heritage* 37 (Spring 2002), 6-31.

[3] A Harvard study led by Diana L Eck, *A New Religious America* (HarperSanFrancisco, 2002), 4, led to the conclusion that "The United States has become the most religiously diverse nation on earth."

[4] H. Richard Niebuhr, *The Purpose of the Church and Its Ministry* (New York, Evanston, and London: Harper & Row, Publishers, 1956), 31.

[5] *George Herbert: The Country Parson, The Temple*, ed. John Wall, Jr. Classics of Western Spirituality (New York, Ramsey, Toronto: Paulist Press, 1981), 316.

[6] Thomas Merton, "The Contemplative Life: Its Meaning and Necessity," *The Dublin Review* 223 (Winter 1949), 27.

[7] Margaret Benefiel, *Soul at Work: Spiritual Leadership in Organizations* (New York: Seabury Books, 2005) cited evidence of spiritual leadership in U2, Sisters of the Road Café, Reell Precision Manufacturing, Greystone Foundation, HealthEast, and Southwest Airlines, businesses in the U.S. and Ireland.

[8] Christopher Hill, *Society and Puritanism in Pre-Revolutionary England* (New York: Schocken Books, 1964, 1967), 449.

[9] Thomas Merton, "Contemplation in a World of Action," in *Contemplation in a World of Action* (Garden City, NJ: Doubleday & Co., Inc., 1971), 164.

[10] Thomas Merton, *The Inner Experience: Notes on Contemplation*, ed. William H. Shannon (HarperSanFrancisco, 2003), 18.

[11] Ibid., 19.

[12] Ibid., 22.

[13] Ibid., 45.

[14] See E. Glenn Hinson, "Expansive Catholicism: Merton's Ecumenical Perceptions," *Cistercian Studies* 48 (Spring 1979), 290-304.

CPSIA information can be obtained at www.ICGtesting.com
Printed in the USA
LVOW100157120613

338071LV00018B/925/P